TRACING YOUR RURAL ANCESTORS

A Guide for Family Historians

JONATHAN BROWN

Pen & Sword
FAMILY HISTORY

First published in Great Britain in 2011 by
PEN AND SWORD FAMILY HISTORY
an imprint of
Pen & Sword Books Ltd
47 Church Street
Barnsley
South Yorkshire
S70 2AS

Copyright © Jonathan Brown 2011

ISBN 978 1 84884 227 4

A CIP catalogue record for this book is
available from the British Library

Typeset in 10pt Palatino by Mac Style, Beverley, East Yorkshire
Printed and bound in the UK by CPI

Pen & Sword Books Ltd incorporates the Imprints of Pen & Sword
Aviation, Pen & Sword Maritime, Pen & Sword Military,
Wharncliffe Local History, Pen and Sword Select, Pen and Sword
Military Classics, Leo Cooper, Remember When, Seaforth Publishing
and Frontline Publishing.

For a complete list of Pen & Sword titles please contact
PEN & SWORD BOOKS LIMITED
47 Church Street, Barnsley, South Yorkshire, S70 2AS, England
E-mail: enquiries@pen-and-sword.co.uk
Website: www.pen-and-sword.co.uk

TRACING YOUR
RURAL ANCESTORS

FAMILY HISTORY FROM PEN & SWORD BOOKS

CONTENTS

Contents

PREFACE

M ost of us probably have rural ancestors. Often they are not that far distant: after all, half the population of England and Wales lived in the country in 1851. My father was from the first generation in his family to leave the village when, after the Second World War, he joined the Post Office telephone service. He went first to the market town. After climbing the telegraph poles in the surrounding villages for a while, he was promoted to head office in London and embarked upon a life in suburbia. His father had been a village baker, and before him there was a complement of agricultural labourers in the family.

Ernest Brown's (my grandfather's) scales. Made in Birmingham, of course, so nothing intrinsically rural about them. (The author)

Such stories can be replicated many times over in families across the land, and tracing something of them can be very rewarding. Frustrating as well, of course, because the trail can so quickly run cold as far as any record with names is concerned. I would be hard pushed to find anything mentioning my grandfather Ernest Brown as a baker, except probably the censuses of the time, and they have not been released yet. He is certainly not in the county directories. But I know that is what he was. Ernest told me a little about it when he was alive. I saw his bakehouse. I have ridden his delivery bike – and fallen off it into a ditch. I have his scales; and I use them to weigh my flour when I make bread.

In a sense I have just been following the first 'rule' of family history – start from what we know about our families, and work out from there. And in this book I shall try to do something similar. If we have names from the census or the parish registers telling us our ancestors were farm labourers or whatever, how do we work outwards from there to the surroundings in which these people lived? So, I shall take a look at the constitution of rural society – the farmers and their workers, the landowners, the village tradesmen, and the professional people – to discover who they were, how they lived, and what records they might have left. The frustrations will remain, for the number of records that mention our rural forebears by name will often be small. But I hope the potential rewards will also be apparent as we discover a bit more about the lives our ancestors lived. The sky, almost, is the limit: potentially there are many avenues to explore in fleshing out the history of our family.

It will not be possible to cover everything in a volume this size. The great variety of regional and local society will of necessity be over-simplified. I shall also have to concentrate only on the village, for to look at the society of the country town in any detail would introduce too many extra paths to explore. But the links between village and market town were too intimate for the town to be completely excluded – after all, many a village could once have been classed as a town, but its market declined.

In what follows, the first chapter gives a brief introduction to the structure and nature of rural society. Later chapters talk about the principal groups of people who might be found in the village, and how they might be described in the documents. These chapters will tend to work backwards from the recent past into earlier centuries, just as when constructing the story of our families. At the end of each is a brief guide to some of the sources in which records of these people can be found.

Chapter 9 lists and describes major types of record that can be useful – and some of their pitfalls – and chapter 10 gives some guidance on where and how to get access to the books and documents. The bibliography offers suggestions for further reading to cover most interests, including books that range from introductory texts to the more detailed and academic.

Many people have contributed to the making of this book – unknowingly, over the time long before my colleague Guy Baxter put the project in my in tray. They include those who have sent me their enquiries relating to their own family research. In answering them their concerns seeped into my thinking. The members of family history and local history groups, and continuing education classes, to whom I have given talks from time to time, have all helped through their questions and responses in the composition of this book. My thanks go to all of these, but one special word must be for my former work colleague Christine Croker. I have listened over a number of years to the tales of her quest for rural ancestors, which took her to the far north-east and almost the far south-west of England, and she has prompted many thoughts for this book.

Chapter 1

THE NATURE OF
COUNTRY SOCIETY

I was talking to a friend one day about where I'd been on holiday. 'Oh, yes,' she said, 'I grew up near there, in a tiny village.' Tiny it certainly is, only a few houses, the kind of place that passing through on holiday you blink and miss it. This serves to remind us, however, that our rural ancestors came from a wide range of backgrounds, from isolated farms, or tiny hamlets of only a few houses, up to villages that had a population larger than some places that could call themselves towns.

My grandparents lived in two such contrasting villages. The baker grandfather lived in a fairly small village – it had a population of 200 in the mid-nineteenth century. Even at this time there were few trades other than farming. Where he lived was a new development that had been built after the railway came; it was detached from the main village – separated by the railway – and had a different feeling to it. It was actually more convenient to go to the shop in the neighbouring village. My other grandparents lived for a while in a village that was very different. This was the village of Heckington, on the edge of the Fens, near Sleaford in Lincolnshire. It is a big place: the parish was six miles long by six miles broad, the directory for 1856 noted, and 1581 people lived there in 1851. Its main claim to fame now is its large eight-sailed windmill, a unique survival.

The local history group produced a book about the village (*Heckington in the Eighteen Seventies*, Heckington Village Trust, 1979), and books such as this can be a useful way to get an introduction to the locality and the rural society in which our ancestors lived. These types of book vary in quality, but there are enough good ones to be well worth looking for in the local studies libraries.

Using the parish returns for the census – one of the main sources for the family historian, of course – this book analyzes the structure of Heckington's population. The village had grown in size since 1851: the census for 1871 recorded 1865 residents of the parish. It was a thoroughly

The eight-sailed windmill at Heckington. It was worked by a family called Pocklington, who were also coal merchants. (Author's collection)

agricultural village. Nearly half (47.71 per cent) of the adult males were recorded as agricultural labourers, and 14 per cent were farmers, farmers' sons or farm bailiffs. Most of the others in work were effectively supporting the farming – the tradesmen and craftsmen, including millers (there were four of them at that time), blacksmiths and wheelwrights.

It was a similar story in another large parish a few miles further north, of which another local study has been made, this time based around the census returns for 1851 (R J Olney, ed, *Labouring Life on the Lincolnshire Wolds,* 1975). Of the working population of Binbrook, in the Lincolnshire Wolds, 47 per cent were agricultural workers, variously described as farm labourers, servants, waggoners and shepherds, of whom more will be said in the next chapter. The next largest group in Binbrook, the craftsmen, presented a similar roll call of blacksmiths and wheelwrights providing services for agriculture as in Heckington. The farmers made up a smaller proportion because the farms in Binbrook were fewer in number and considerably larger than those in Heckington.

Of the other working people, the next largest group was the retailers, taken in a broad sense – the tailors, boot and shoemakers, dressmakers. Then there were the building trades – builders, bricklayers, carpenters. Other groups in the population included the professional people – teachers, solicitors, and the like – and those of independent means. These were all a very small proportion of the whole. Very few people were described as retired – only five in Binbrook in 1851 and sixteen in Heckington in 1871 – one of many ways in which this society differs from that of a century later. Not very many were entered as paupers or on parish relief.

Of course, these are but two examples among the thousands of rural parishes, of all shapes and sizes. They are not intended to present a general description of rural England, merely to show in broad outline the types of people we can expect to find when we start examining family and local history in the countryside. These two villages were in a very agricultural part of the country, whereas in other areas there might be villages with more crafts and trades, quarries and industries less directly connected with farming. Nevertheless, until the late nineteenth century farming was the largest part of village life almost everywhere. National figures show that, including landowners, about a quarter of males aged above twenty were employed in agriculture in 1851.

The types of study represented by Binbrook and Heckington are snapshots in time. As a result there are a number of aspects of rural life that they do not show fully. One is the fluidity of rural society, which is not fully reflected in such sources as the census returns. A village family was likely to embrace a number of occupations. The Enticknap family of Kirdford, Sussex, in the second half of the nineteenth century included a blacksmith, a shoemaker, a farm labourer and a small farmer. While some crafts needed application and were likely to occupy people for some years, there was considerable movement from one occupation to another. My grandfather gave up being a baker after a lengthy illness and became a postman. Many of the villagers were likely to work part time at a number of trades, the butcher having a little land and engaging in a bit of general trading, for example.

The second thing that the snapshot does not show is how changes affected rural life from age to age. Heckington's population of 1865 in 1871 represented a substantial increase compared with previous censuses. The first census in 1801 had recorded 1042 people. The figure for 1871, however, was the high-water mark for the nineteenth century; thereafter Heckington's population declined until the second half of the twentieth century.

This was a common phenomenon of the nineteenth century, experienced throughout rural England. The effects of industrialization and urbanization were taking so many of our ancestors away from the countryside that the total population of rural England recorded a decline of a million, from 8.9m to 7.9m, between 1851 and 1911. In some of the more rural counties of England – including Cambridgeshire, Norfolk, Huntingdonshire, Wiltshire and Somerset – the local towns were not large enough to counteract the decline in village populations. As a result the total population in these counties recorded a decline from 1861 onwards.

In the villages the experience of Heckington was typical – indeed many reached their peak far sooner in the century, as early as the 1820s for a few. More common was a peak reached about mid-century, with a rapid decline in village populations between the 1850s and 1870s. In Oxfordshire, there were many villages that experienced rising population until the middle decades of the century; the decline that followed was so sharp that some villages, such as Cuxham, Peasemore and Shillingford, ended the nineteenth century with smaller populations than they had in 1801. Stifford, on the southern marshes of Essex, increased in population during the first half of the nineteenth century. Decline then set in, but unlike some other places this was halted in 1891 when the spread of suburbanization from London began to make itself felt.

The main driving force behind this movement from the villages was the attraction of urban employment, for in the 1850s-60s, when so many were moving away to the towns, demand for labour in agriculture was still strong. There were complaints of labour shortages, but they counted for little when the agricultural labourer's wage of perhaps 15s a week,

Landlords built improved cottages in the mid-nineteenth century to try and counteract the loss of labour resulting from migration away from the village. This is an example from Berkshire. (Author's collection)

and often less, was easily surpassed in the town. However, the decline in the rural population became a great concern to contemporaries at the end of the nineteenth century. Journalists and scholars would write articles about the 'rural exodus' and a 'flight from the land' until more pressing concerns took over.

The effect of industrialization, a rising national population and these movements away from rural England combined to shift the balance between town and country. At the 1901 census 20 per cent of the total population was reckoned as rural, and 80 per cent urban; in 1851 the proportions were 50:50; whereas in 1801, when the first census was taken, 80 per cent of the population was rural, 20 per cent urban

The break with agriculture was taking hold at the same time. By 1901 the proportion of the working population engaged in farming was down to 10 per cent. As a proportion of the total population, agriculture's share was even smaller. The total number of people in England and Wales was 35.5 million when Edward VII came to the throne in 1901. The number of farmers was about 225,000, a small fraction of that total. Adding the members of the farmer's family, the farm workers, contractors and others brought the total engaged in agriculture to about 1.2 million.

These changes during the second half of the nineteenth century represent one of the greatest breaks with the past, for the 1801 census recorded a position that had been maintained for many centuries. Until the Industrial Revolution got under way, the population of England and Wales lived mostly in the country. In 1700 three out of four people lived in the countryside, and most of them were more or less directly involved in agriculture. At least 60 per cent of the total population calculated by Gregory King in 1688 were so employed. An increase in the total population of England from about 5.8 million to 16.7 million during the course of the eighteenth century did little to change that. Nor did the first stages in the Industrial Revolution during the eighteenth century have much immediate effect, for many of the new workshops were in the countryside and powered by water.

Rural migration

Migration from country to town was not a new phenomenon – the tale of Dick Whittington was an old one – but industrialization gave it added impetus and volume. There was considerable movement of people within the countryside as well. Most of it was over a short distance. The census returns reveal something of the way our rural ancestors moved from parish to parish. At the 1871 census only 39 per cent of Heckington's population were natives of the village itself. However, 84 per cent had been born within a radius of twenty miles of the parish. It was a similar story at Binbrook in 1851: 89 per cent came from within twenty miles, and slightly less than half the population (600 out of 1269) were born in Binbrook.

Records of the Act of Settlement – licences and removal orders – also show rural dwellers moving short distances for work. Typical were those who moved the distance of seven miles or so from Earley, south east of Reading, to Tilehurst, on the western side of the town; both are now suburban areas, but in the nineteenth century they were distinct country settlements. Many of these movements were short-term as well, people moving on, or back after only a few years. The ten-year interval of the census sometimes obscures such movements. It was by such short steps, rather than in one long journey, that many migrants reached the towns.

There were many exceptions to this rule, especially after the railway made it easier to travel across country. People left the poorer agricultural southern counties to find better-paid work in the mines and factories of the north. Emigration provides a further example of long-distance migration. Members of all classes of rural society left for the United States and the British colonies in considerable numbers. Farmers, and especially younger sons, sought better prospects abroad. In the early nineteenth century there were implement-makers offering 'emigrants' packs' to help the departing farmer set himself up in his new land. Labourers also moved abroad. Societies to promote emigration were formed in the early nineteenth century. Some raised funds to help poor emigrants, and parish overseers sometimes did the same. Later on, the first agricultural trade unions also encouraged emigration, partly because they thought that a reduced supply of labour in the village might raise wages for those that remained. Besides the free migrants, there were some who went abroad unwillingly, sentenced to transportation.

Chapter 2

WHO WAS WHO ON THE FARM? THE LABOURERS

As one reads through the nineteenth-century census returns for rural parishes the most common entry for occupation is usually agricultural labourer. There they are, line after line of them. The census enumerators regularly used 'Ag Lab' as an abbreviation. With more than 40 per cent of the male population of the village so employed, as was seen in the last chapter, that is hardly surprising, nor does it come as a surprise that agricultural labourers often feature among our rural ancestors.

According to the census for 1851 there were more than a million farm labourers in England and Wales out of a total population of nearly 18m. The grand total of 1,460,896 was made up of:

outdoor labourers	1,002,728 male
	70,899 female
farm servants	235,943 male
	128,251 female
shepherds	19,075

Figures are hard to come by before the nineteenth century, and it is not a straightforward matter to compare them with the census returns, but it is certain that the labouring population grew during the eighteenth and nineteenth centuries. Gregory King made one of the first estimates of the population of the modern era in 1688, in which he gave a figure of about 1.25 million for the group he called labourers and out-servants. The increase in numbers of labourers up to 1851 was probably greater than a simple comparison between Gregory King and the census suggests, as other local studies have shown. At Moreton Say, in Shropshire, in 1700–5 labourers made up 42 per cent of the population; that proportion had grown to 84 per cent by 1813–22.

This, the period of the Agricultural Revolution, was a time of growing demand for labour in farming, and an increase in the total population of

This is Jack Fillpot. He worked for A Stratton as farm bailiff or foreman at Alton Priors, Wiltshire. The photograph was taken about 1910. (Museum of English Rural Life)

the countryside enabled much of the demand to be met. There were, however, some people who had been counted as independent cottagers who were joining the ranks of agricultural labourers.

From the mid-nineteenth century, however, the numbers of farm labourers fell rapidly: down to 635,000 in 1911. The total of 685,000 in the census for 1921 might represent something of an increase as a result of the First World War, but it also includes more casual workers than before. The downward trend was continuing, however: by 1939 the total of all labourers was 511,000. There was another increase in the labour force during the Second World War, but by 1949 that had been shaken off and the total number of workers, full-time, part-time and casual, stood at 490,000. In 1980 there were 255,000.

All of this is saying that until recent times the agricultural labourers were common figures in village life and it is useful to find out who these people were. It is worth noting at this point that when someone is described simply as labourer in the parish census, he is probably not a farm worker. The census enumerators generally were good at distinguishing between agricultural labourers and those employed, say, by the building contractor.

The farm labouring population was far from homogeneous. Some were specialists, others more general workers, and there were many different descriptions of the workers and their work.

Specialist workers

There was a hierarchy amongst the labourers on the farm. The shepherds were reckoned to be at the top, for sheep husbandry had enjoyed status in English farming for centuries. The independence of the shepherd also set him apart. The horsemen might dispute that precedence, however, and on some more arable farms it is arguable that they did hold the top rank. Certainly they held a senior status. If there was a farm foreman, he more often than not was appointed from the ranks of the horsemen.

The men who worked with the horses were usually specialists; the man at the head of the stables certainly was, although some of those who assisted him in the fields may have been ordinary labourers. These specialist horsemen were styled differently in various parts of the country. In the north-east of Scotland, for example, they were called simply horsemen, as they were in Essex and Suffolk. In Suffolk they might also be known as baiters. In Kent they were usually referred to as waggoners. There were also waggoners in the east Midlands and Lincolnshire,

A shepherd leading his flock through the lanes of Burnham, Buckinghamshire in the 1930s. (Museum of English Rural Life)

although horseman was also used. Carter was another common term, used throughout most of southern England, and ploughman another widespread name. Less common was teamsman, the style used in Cheshire and Lancashire. Whatever they were called, these were the men who walked miles as they went up and down the field behind the plough.

The workers with cattle had lower status. They were variously described as cattleman, byreman, or garth man. Dairymen and dairymaids were the ones who worked in the milking parlour and were involved in the handling of the milk in the dairy. Dairyman might also be used to refer to a dairy farmer, especially one who sold his milk by retail.

On large farms there was likely to be further hierarchy, most clearly seen within the ranks of the horsemen. The head horseman was answerable to the farmer or his foreman, and under him came the second horseman, third horseman ('second chap' and 'third chap') and so on down to the junior ploughboy. On large farms six or seven horsemen were not unusual, with two or three lads who generally did the light jobs until they were old enough and strong enough to take on ploughing. Precedence was rigidly maintained: the head horseman's authority over the stables was unquestioned. He passed the farmer's orders on down the line of horsemen, and expected the respect due to his position. The head horseman always had the best horses, and he led in everything, however small. He was the first to enter the yard in the morning, first to feed his horses, first to harness, and so on with every step through the day.

Hiring fairs

Most of those specialist workers – the horsemen, shepherds, cowmen and dairymaids – were employed by annual agreement. The hiring fair – or statute fair (so called after the Statute of Labourers of 1387) – was the occasion for agreements to be struck. It was held in the market town; those seeking employment would stand in the market place, and, to advertise their trade, the waggoner had a whip in his hand and the shepherd his crook. There they would await the approach of prospective employers. When the bargain had been struck the farmer gave his new workman a token payment, the 'fasten penny'. In the nineteenth century most statute fairs were reported in the local papers. Individuals were not reported upon, unless they met with an accident or misbehaved at the fair, but this is a source for general comment, and for some fairs an indication of the wages being paid. At Gainsborough's May hiring fair in 1879, it was reported that foremen were being hired for £20–24 a year, waggoners for £15–18, lads for £7-10 and 'girls to milk' for £7-9. (*Stamford Mercury*, 23 May 1879)

Most of these fairs were held in May or October, and there was often a little succession of them at these seasons, which gave a second or third opportunity for those who had not found a job. In some places there were 'runaway' fairs a fortnight or so after the main one, for farm servants (and their employers) had a couple of weeks to decide if the new situation was not for them. At Dorchester in Dorset the hiring fair was held outside these main seasons, on Old Candlemas Day – 14 February. Thomas Hardy described the fair in *Far From the Madding Crowd*, published in 1874:

At one end of the street stood from two to three hundred blithe and hearty labourers waiting upon Chance – all men of the

17

stamp to whom labour suggests nothing worse than a wrestle with gravitation, and nothing better than a renunciation of the same. Among these, carters and waggoners were distinguished by having a piece of whip-cord twisted round their hats; thatchers wore a fragment of woven straw; shepherds held their sheep-crooks in their hands; and thus the situation required was known to the hirers at a glance.

The hiring fair was a great occasion, a day off for all those employed through these annual contracts. William Marshall, one of the leading writers on agriculture at the end of the eighteenth century, described the day of the statutes in west Sussex: 'The roads were crowded with farm servants, leaving their places and hying to the fair. It was a complete holiday: not a team to be seen; or a stroke of work going forward.' He did not approve of such levity, and nor did lots of other people. They regarded the hiring fair as an excuse for excess, with workers on their day off finding release in the fun of the fair as well as the business of getting a new job. This sense of propriety led to attempts to control the fairs. The decline in employment by annual contract, and changes in employment practices for hiring those that were still employed thus, were having a greater effect. Registry offices acting as employment agencies and local newspapers were providing an alternative means for workers to find employment. There was increasing use of written agreements of employment rather than the shaking of hands at the fair.

By the 1870s the hiring fair was in decline; a typical item in a local newspaper reported in this manner:

> Monday last was the statute for hiring servants, and the contrast between what Spilsby Statute used to be half a century ago and what it now is was most marked … Now very few young persons of the servant class attend, most of them having already made their engagements. (*Stamford Mercury*, 1 May 1874)

The fair might have been declining in importance, but it was in no hurry to go altogether. Even in the southern counties, where it was declining the fastest, there were many, like Dorchester's, still in existence as the nineteenth century drew to its close. The numbers attending were smaller, however, and by the 1890s fewer workers wore the token of their trade; they dressed in a suit rather than a smock. The pleasure-fair part of

A hiring agreement between A Deacon, farmer, and A W Pembroke, carter, of Aldbourne, Wiltshire, for a year's work from October 1912. (Museum of English Rural Life)

proceedings was gaining greater prominence, and this is the form in which some of the statute fairs continue still.

The tradition of hiring through the fairs was strongest in the more northern areas of England, and the custom was still alive into the twentieth century. Not far from the Lincolnshire town of Spilsby, the Gainsborough statutes were reported as doing good business in 1890. In not a few places in this county hiring for the year continued for as long as horses were used. Between the wars there were still numbers of horsemen living in. Near Boston, for example, there were young men being lodged with the farm foreman in the 1920s. The practice had not entirely died out by the beginning of the Second World War. Sometimes this continued even beyond 1945.

Farm servants

In the mid-nineteenth century census returns, those people hired by the year were the ones distinguished as farm servants (indoors).

By 'farm servant' the census meant employees who were boarded by the employer, most often in the farmhouse, but sometimes in an outhouse, or perhaps billeted with the farm foreman. In some parts of the country these might be referred to as 'confined men'. Young single people were most often employed in this way. They might also be described as servants, maids and boys. Boys and girls might enter farm service between the ages of twelve and fifteen. The initial arrangement was usually between the parents and the prospective employer. This was common in many walks of life – domestic service, for example – and was how Laura came to leave Lark Rise to enter service in the Post Office in Flora Thompson's *Lark Rise to Candleford*. After this initial engagement the servants could move of their own accord, finding work through the hiring fair or other arrangement.

The farmhouse could be quite a full place, especially in the more remote districts, where indoor servants were most common. Two farmhouses in the parish of Cottam in the Yorkshire Wolds contained forty-one people between them at the 1841 census. Further north, at Blindburn Farm in Northumberland, the household in 1841 included the farmer, his wife, three shepherds, a retired shepherd aged eighty, five children, and six farm servants – seventeen people in all. With the three neighbouring farms there were thirty-six people resident where now there are five.

The remoteness of farms such as Blindburn encouraged the widespread use of farm service in Northumberland, where it was commonly known as the 'bondage' system. The young farm servants lived in the farm or in blocks of cottages immediately at hand and were paid mainly in kind. The workers were often referred to as bondmen and women; 'hind' was the other common term used in this region for the male worker, and 'cottar' was the female worker. In these northern counties there was also a custom of hiring families as a whole. The head of the household – usually the hind, but there were 'cottar' hirings when a widow was head of the household – agreed to work on the farm for the year, bringing his family with him to the cottage provided, whose members would also work in different capacities. This was how James Nixon hired himself to Sir Edward Blackett at Hatton Hall Farm in 1865. He was to earn 16s 6d a week, in addition to his cottage, and his son would have work for half the year at 9s, and his daughters would be found work at the discretion of the farm steward. This type of hiring was still to be found at the end of the nineteenth century.

The farm servants were hired, and paid, by the year, and there was often an element of supplementary payment in kind – coal allowance, for example. At the year's end they were free to move on, and many did: study of parish records can reveal the frequency with which farm servants moved. As has been seen, the hiring fair was the common way for finding a new situation until it was supplanted by other means such as newspaper advertisements.

When they got married the young man's or woman's employment as an indoor servant usually came to an end. There were older, married horsemen and cattlemen, still paid by annual agreement but living in a cottage provided by the farm or estate or one they rented privately, and the term 'farm servant' was still applied to them in many quarters. However, for most farm lads, marriage meant that they not only ceased to live in, but they became ordinary day labourers. It was at this point in their careers that many in the nineteenth century were likely to move to new employment, as often as not away from the farm. If they stayed in the countryside they might get work with a threshing contractor, on the local railway or with the police. They were just as likely to move to the towns or take a job in the pit. Fred Kitchen, a farm labourer in the West Riding of Yorkshire, went to the mines, as he recounted in his autobiography *Brother to the Ox*.

In the census returns only those living in were described as farm servants: any who retained their annual hiring after marriage were counted as labourers. There remained also some confusion in the census returns between the figures recorded for female farm servants and domestic servants, even of farmers' relatives.

In the seventeenth and eighteenth centuries farm servants were a high proportion of the agricultural work force – between a third and a half. They were always most numerous in the more remote parts of the country, such as Northumberland and the Wolds of Yorkshire and Lincolnshire: even as late as the 1870s more than 40 per cent of the labourers were farm servants in such places. In general, however, farm servants were in decline by the nineteenth century. Since the second half of the eighteenth century farmers had been finding the costs of boarding farm servants too high, and started turning to other conditions of employment for their labour force. In the 1851 census farm servants were 17 per cent of the total number of agricultural workers, although the census definition might have been more restrictive than common use. Nevertheless the proportion of workers employed in this way was clearly falling, and it led the census to drop the distinction between indoor and outdoor labourers from 1871 onwards.

Outdoor labourers

The second broad category in the mid-nineteenth century census returns was the agricultural labourer (outdoors). By this was meant those who lived out of the farmhouse. Most of those who fell into this category were the general labourers, commonly called day labourers in the nineteenth century, the ones at the bottom of the hierarchy in farm labour. In census terms, however, a few of the specialist workers – those who lived off the farm – might fall within the class of outdoor servants.

These general labourers made up the majority of workers on the farm. According to the census for Dorset, for example, in 1891 there were 11,282 agricultural labourers compared with only 716 shepherds and 1226 horsemen.

The term of their hiring was most often by the day – hence the common term 'day labourer' to describe them. This meant that loss of a day's work for any reason resulted in no pay for the day, and when times were hard for the farmer he was sometimes keen to enforce that rule. Payment of the wage, of course, came at the end of the week. Day labourers did not live on the farm, but in cottages not directly attached to the farm, often in the main part of the village. Many of the cottages, however, were provided by the landed estate that owned the farm – indeed many estates, anxious to improve living conditions for labourers, were building new cottages during the mid-nineteenth century. The idealistic Dorothea in George Eliot's *Middlemarch* was full of schemes for building model cottages on her uncle's estate. The cottages owned by the estate were often managed through the farmers, thus giving rise to the 'tied cottage' system that gained notoriety through twentieth-century trade union campaigns.

Farm labourers were never well paid, and often amongst the poorest of village society. One of the demands of the 'Swing' rioters of 1830 in southern England was that labourers' wages should be increased to 2s per day. Pay was especially low in the south where there was little competition for labour from industry. In the Midlands and north of England wages were higher – by half as much again compared to Dorset or Sussex – but still not particularly good. A number of things followed from this. First, many labourers simply gave up and followed better prospects, most of them away from the countryside. Second, farm labouring families were quite likely to find themselves in dire straits, and featuring in records relating to poor relief, on which more will be said in chapter 8. A third and more positive aspect was that nineteenth-century labourers went in for some self-help, establishing sick clubs and friendly societies, and the records of some of these may survive (see chapter 7).

Casual workers

There were a number of independent agricultural workers who went from farm to farm doing such jobs as hedging, for which special skills might be required. They were a very small part of the labour force in farming, but were of some significance nonetheless. They enjoyed higher status than ordinary labourers by virtue of their skills, and often had better education and with that greater income.

Joseph Arch was one of these men. He was a full-time specialist hedger in the 1840s; his skills won him many prizes, including Champion Hedgecutter of England. 'I got good jobs and very good money, and was in great request,' he wrote in his autobiography (*The Story of His Life Told by Himself,* 1898). His work took him on travels through several English and Welsh counties from his home in Warwickshire, experience that was to prove useful when he became leader of the National Agricultural Labourers Union in the 1870s. He was unusual in rising to prominence and in having an autobiography published; most hedgers left little record, but the competitions were an important part of their lives – they still are – and were reported in the local press, while prize certificates might turn up in family papers.

Other skilled specialist farm workers were thatchers, mowers and sheep shearers. The thatchers in this context were the ones who thatched the ricks of hay and corn stacks rather than those who put roofs on buildings. There was overlap between the two, but thatching stacks was a special skill that could afford employment to many a man. Such people travelled a range of territory: some stayed relatively local, whereas others covered great distances. Sheep shearers were perhaps the most-travelled: by the second half of the nineteenth century the shearers from Australia and New Zealand were a common seasonal feature of the farming scene.

Much of the itinerant and casual farm labour was unskilled, and these workers were employed particularly at harvest time. Haytime and, even more, the corn harvest demanded as much labour as could be found. Village women, tradesmen, gypsies, folk from the towns were all drawn into the labour force. Industrial workers would leave their factories for a while to help in the seasonal farm work. In the eighteenth century this was fairly easily done, as many of the mills were still in rural areas and worked by water power. As the factories grew and their sites became more urban, so fewer workers were able to join the farm workforce even for a while. In areas where small farms were common, neighbours would help each other. In many parts of Wales the farmers and their families would turn out to help neighbours with threshing. At haytime and harvest labourers would move around a neighbourhood, often covering quite considerable distances between districts to take advantage of the time lag between different harvest times. In Yorkshire there was about a month's difference between the early harvests in the Humber valley and cutting the crops of the more northern districts, making it an attractive proposition to workers able to go from one end of the county to another.

Irish harvesters were a particular feature of the harvest labour force of the eighteenth and nineteenth centuries. They had started coming across at least from the late seventeenth century and steadily grew in numbers. Groups of men set out from Ireland and steadily worked their way across the country, tackling the hay harvests of Lancashire and Cheshire, moving on to the hay and corn harvests of midland counties, and then to eastern England to cut the cereals. Their arrival was eagerly anticipated, so great was the demand, even dependency upon them in some of the cereal-growing counties. Local newspapers reported their progress:

> There have been more Irish harvestmen in Stamford this summer than for three or four years past, and notwithstanding the almost general use of machine reapers, their services have been in demand in the neighbourhood. (*Stamford Mercury*, 15 August 1873)

By the time of this newspaper report the migration of Irish harvestmen had long passed its peak, estimated at 75,000 a year immediately after the famine of 1846–7. The introduction of machinery ultimately led to the demise of these itinerant harvesters.

While there are copious references to the casual and migrant workers from newspapers and official reports, tracing individuals is less easy as few will have made their mark, unless they perpetrated a misdemeanour bringing them before the magistrates. However, the migratory nature of some of the rural labour force can account for changes that might occur in our family ancestry, as every now and again a young man settles in one of the places he has been working, perhaps marrying a local girl.

There is one big exception: the annual migrations to the hop harvest of Kent and Sussex. 'Hopping down in Kent' is celebrated in songs and literature, such as George Orwell's novel *A Clergyman's Daughter* of 1935. But more, because it continued until after the Second World War into the era of universal schooling and oral history, there are more detailed personal accounts to be found about it. Two of the books about the Kentish hop pickers based on oral history evidence are listed in the bibliography. The hoppers were nearly all Londoners, so the extent to which we discover our rural ancestors through them might be limited, but they were part of an interaction between town and country.

Women's work

According to census figures, there were 143,000 female agricultural labourers in England and Wales in 1851. This was a very small number compared with the million or so male workers. There are, however, many reasons to question the accuracy of the census figures and to suspect that there was some under-recording. Women's work in agriculture was certainly important, and much of it was full time. A farmer in Dorset told the Poor Law Commissioners in 1843, 'I employ six to eight women all the year round; in the winter in threshing and hacking turnips for sheep; at other times in hoeing turnips and keeping land clean, in hay-harvest and corn-harvest.' Thomas Hardy in 1883 commented on women working in the threshing gang, also in Dorset, which was evidently a county where women workers were quite regularly employed in the

Women singling a crop on the farm of J Wadlow in Shropshire, May 1940. (Museum of English Rural Life)

nineteenth century. In other areas, such as East Anglia, far fewer women were employed in farm work.

Female agricultural labour was declining during the nineteenth century, certainly full-time. A number of influences were at work. To some extent mechanization was taking away jobs that had been done by women, in the harvest field, for example. Changing social attitudes were also important. Many thought it was not right for women to be engaged in hard field work; they should be employed about the home, and labourers shared in this rise in feelings of respectability. In *Lark Rise to Candleford*, Flora Thompson wrote that 'any work outside the home was considered unwomanly' as such ideas gained hold in the village. One thing that contributed to this was the uncovering of exploitation of gang workers, which provoked outrage, public enquiry and legislation to curtail the practice, and this especially affected the employment of women.

However, women's work in agriculture certainly did not disappear altogether. Casual work remained for example in singling roots, and the harvests for hay, cereals, and potatoes.

The Women's Land Army

During the First and Second World Wars demand for labour outstripped supply. Men left the land for the armed forces when ploughing-up of pasture land for arable required more workers. One of the most prominent expedients to meet the need was the Women's Land Army. It was created in 1916, a relatively modest organization that did not reach its planned total of 25,000 workers before the armistice in 1918. It was successful enough to be re-instituted in June 1939 in anticipation of the outbreak of war. In September 1939 the Women's Land Army was already 17,000 strong; a peak was reached in 1943 of 87,000.

It can be argued that the Women's Land Army does not strictly count for rural ancestry. Most of its members were from the towns. But they were undoubtedly an important feature of the countryside for a few years, and some settled in the village.

Labour mobility

Mention has been made in chapter 1 of migration within and away from rural society. Those who remained on the land as labourers were far from static in their careers. The young and single, especially, moved from farm to farm; the system of hiring by the year offered an opportunity to the workers to move at the end of the year, and a good many took it.

P DX 879/2

Name Miss M. Swingler

No. 53930

You are now a member of the Women's Land Army.

You are pledged to hold yourself available for service on the land for the period of the war.

You have promised to abide by the conditions of training and employment of the Women's Land Army ; its good name is in your hands.

You have made the home fields your battlefield. Your country relies on your loyalty and welcomes your help.

Signed G. Denman.
                                    Honorary Director

Signed Ada M Palmer
                                    Chairman
                                    Committee

Date 6 · 10 · 41

I realise the national importance of the work which I have undertaken and I will serve well and faithfully.

Signed Marjorie M. Swingler

Membership ticket issued to a new member of the Women's Land Army in 1941. (Museum of English Rural Life)

By the twentieth century labour mobility was increasing. Among the records at the Museum of English Rural Life is an unpublished autobiography written by Bill Petch, who worked as a farm labourer for most of his life between the 1930s and 1970s. Bill was a native of

Hertfordshire, but his career took him round the country to work at various times in East Anglia, Sussex, Staffordshire, Wiltshire, Oxfordshire, Hampshire and Berkshire. He was far from alone in such mobility. One of his employers was Joe Lawson of St Neots in Huntingdonshire. This farmer had a complement of five or six men; in the five years that Bill worked there, fifty-six men passed through. Some stayed for years, but many for only a matter of weeks. One only lasted two days.

Twentieth-century change

In 1908 a new trade union was formed, the National Union of Agricultural Workers. Many of the founders and leaders of that union had a broadly socialist philosophy, and it was they who decided to adopt the word 'worker' in the title rather than 'labourer', which was still the more generally used term. Under their influence 'agricultural labourer' was turned into a term rather of abuse – the symbol of the downtrodden latter-day serf. Gradually labourers began to be called agricultural workers, or preferably farm workers. Another older term, farmhand, which had been more common in American usage than British, was also gaining ground.

It took a long time for 'worker' to take hold, though. Probably most of those working on farms before the Second World War quite happily called themselves labourers still. Hugh Barrett, in his autobiographical book *A Good Living*, about his life as farm manager and farmer, comments on a farm in Shropshire where he worked during the Second World War. 'There were tractor drivers,' he writes, 'a few general labourers (these were the days before "labourers" became "workers" or "craftsmen") who did the basic cultivations, and with them was a very large almost permanent gang of women.'

The nature of farm work was changing as rapidly as the numbers in the workforce. The end of the horse economy on the farm finally put an end to the remnants of the farm service culture and living in, which had lingered in some places beyond 1945. The establishment of wages boards also had an effect on the farm structure.

The specialist terms were changing too, as byremen and garthmen became stockmen. Advertisements in *Farmer & Stockbreeder* in the early 1920s show this transition at work, as we find positions for carters and ploughmen advertised alongside newer terms such as pigman, cowman, herdsman. Soon tractor driver replaced horseman. But something of the established hierarchy on the farm remained, for the tractor driver tended to replace the horseman at the top of the tree.

Bill Petch talks of labourers coming from more varied backgrounds in the twentieth century: 'Until 1939 son followed father, but now farmhands have varied backgrounds: when I went to a farm in Wiltshire in the sixties a previous cowman had named the cows from the letters of the Greek alphabet.' Workers were better educated, not only through the elementary schools but often, like Bill, going to agricultural college.

In the 1980s Neil Carter lost his job as pigman at Brookfield Farm, in the radio programme *The Archers*. One of his subsequent jobs was with an agricultural contractor, and in this he was part of a trend, for many of those who had left the employ of the farmer continued in agricultural work. They joined the contractors, who were taking an increasing part in the work of the farm. There had been contracting firms in threshing and steam ploughing since the nineteenth century, but by the mid-twentieth they had taken on almost all aspects of arable farming, from ploughing to combine harvesting, while livestock farmers could employ contractors for their milking, pig work and other stock handling.

Trade unions

The village of Tolpuddle in Dorset has achieved fame as the place where in 1831 a group of farm labourers was convicted of unlawful association and sentenced to transportation to Australia. Their group has been celebrated as the earliest trade union for rural workers, and the six men convicted as martyrs for the cause of workers' rights. Their proto-union, however, did not survive long: the law and society were against them, and it was not until the 1870s that further trade union activity for agricultural labourers got off the ground. A number of local associations were started, and a bigger National Agricultural Labourers Union was founded in 1872, led by Joseph Arch.

This national union and most of its local contemporaries were short-lived. The union struck for better wages in 1873–4, a contest which sapped its strength, and the unions soon declined. It was not until the foundation of the National Union of Agricultural Workers in 1908 that a stronger, more permanent organization was established. This union continued in independent existence until it merged with the Transport and General Workers Union in 1982.

Unfortunately, very few records survive from the nineteenth-century trades unions. Matters improve with the National Union of Agricultural Workers, the records of which survive in greater quantity (for details see chapter 9). All in all, it is not the most profitable line of enquiry for records of individual labourers.

Sources for farm labourers

Agricultural labourers from earlier centuries have, on the whole, created relatively few records themselves. Education and economic growth changed that to quite an extent, so that the memorabilia of a farm worker of the late nineteenth and twentieth centuries can be as extensive as for any other people. Letters, photographs, union membership cards, prizes at ploughing matches – all may be included amongst personal effects. Some have gone further and, like Bill Petch, recorded their life's experiences, either on paper or on tape. A few examples have been found from the nineteenth century. John Burnett included extracts from an autobiography written by Tom Mullins, a farm labourer, later farmer, from Cheshire, in his book *Useful Toil*. Some of these accounts by labourers have been published.

By their nature, such memorabilia do not always survive. To build up a fuller picture of the life of our labouring ancestors we have to move to other sources. Maps of the area in which they worked, for example, help set the context for their lives. Sometimes the records of the farmers who employed them survive, which record dates of employment and wages paid. In the absence of those records, other useful sources can include local newspapers, with their reports on hiring fairs and other farm activities, and official sources, such as select committee and Royal Commission reports. The report of the Select Committee on Labourers' Wages (Parliamentary Papers, vol. vi, 1824) is just one example.

Contemporary books on farming and rural society can be useful background. The series of reports produced by the Board of Agriculture at the end of the eighteenth century and beginning of the nineteenth included a few pages on labour, with information on the wages paid to them and their cottages, for example. They are often called 'General views', from their common title, such as Charles Vancouver's *General View of the Agriculture of the County of Devon* (1808). Sir Frederick Eden's *The State of the Poor* sometimes goes into more detail about the lives of labourers.

Even fully employed, the labourers were among the poorest of rural society, and the records of the poor laws and laws of settlement thus become potential sources, as do the manorial court rolls in which administrative and legal matters affecting them were recorded.

Labourers were as likely as anybody to find themselves before the magistrates, mainly for such petty misdemeanours as being drunk and disorderly, but occasionally on a more serious charge. Poaching was a common offence. Most of this was of a casual nature: systemic poachers were more or less professional. The records of quarter sessions and other criminal courts, therefore, can be additional sources for labouring ancestors.

Records for the Women's Land Army are scattered. The National Archives has index cards to service records of members of the Land Army between 1939 and 1948. That does not give the complete record of service, but it does confirm names of those who were members; it is available as a microform copy only. There is no equivalent for the First World War. Other documents, photographs, newsletters, oral history recordings and uniforms can be found in many places, from the national collections in the Imperial War Museum to local museums and record offices.

Chapter 3

THE FARMERS OF
OLD ENGLAND

Farmers

A ccording to Gregory King's estimates in 1688 there were more people who might be termed farmers than there were labourers – the freeholders and tenants totalled about 1.75m. By 1851 there were approximately three times as many labourers as farmers.

Perusal of the nineteenth-century directories and parish census returns shows us that in many villages farmers were often the biggest group in what might be called the trading and professional classes. Elsewhere, if they were not the biggest, they were generally amongst the leading groups of the parish. This was a situation that prevailed until well into the twentieth century, despite a decline in the numbers of farmers.

That decline had followed the great agricultural depression of the late nineteenth century. From nearly 250,000 farmers in England and Wales in 1871 the number fell to 225,000 in 1901 and to less than 209,000 in 1911. Before this time the number of farmers seems to have been remarkably stable. The census started recording farmers as an occupation in 1841, and all the figures until 1871 were a little below 250,000. Making comparisons with estimates of numbers from earlier periods is not straightforward. The figure I mentioned at the beginning of the chapter, taken from Gregory King's work of 1688, is much higher than the census returns. But on another reading of King's figures we get a number of farmers much closer to the 1841 census. A lot depends on what people may be classed as farmers: there were several different descriptions, especially of small-scale farmers, as we shall see shortly.

The decline in numbers of the late nineteenth century had an impact on village society, as the agricultural depression and other economic developments caused some to leave farming and discouraged others from taking it up. There were, for example, 1,988 farmers in Berkshire according to the census for 1861. By 1891 farmers were down to 1,486, and to 1,347 by 1911. Most of these farmers were men, but women constituted a noticeable minority: 165 of the total in Berkshire were women in 1861. Almost all of those will have been widows, technically holding the farm on behalf of a son yet to come of age. Most of the farmers also were married: from the 1861 census, again, 1,294 were married. Most of those without a wife would have been widowers. On the whole, landowners were not keen to let to a single farmer, and for most farmers the marriage partnership was a practical and working one.

Those census figures alone reveal relatively little, for farmers were far from being a homogeneous group. The figures for farm sizes present a sharply tapering pyramid, with a small number of large holdings and a great number of small ones. Continuing with our sample from Berkshire, in 1875 there were ten farm holdings returned as being more than 1,000 acres, 395 were between 300 and 1,000 acres, 643 between 100 and 300 acres, and 2,983 holdings of less than 100 acres. There were more than twice as many farms as there were farmers. Part of the explanation is that many of the smallest holdings, of less than fifty acres, were held by people not reckoned as farmers, something to which we shall return. At the same time there were many farmers with more than one farm holding. This affected all sizes of farm holding, from the small to very large.

Some farmers had vast acreages under their command as a result. George Baylis of Wyfield Manor, near Newbury, built up a farming enterprise of several thousand acres on the Downs: with 3,440 acres it was already large in 1896, but by 1917 there were 12,140 acres. Baylis was a particularly striking example, unusual in the extent of his farm enterprise, but he was far from the only one to hold large farms in multiple. Berkshire may broadly be said to be a county of large-scale farming. To take the 1875 returns of farm sizes again, but this time for acreages, 54 per cent of the total acreage was in holdings of more than 300 acres, 32 per cent in the middling farms of 100 to 300 acres, and 14 per cent in small farms.

At the upper reaches of the farming ladder were those men controlling great acreages. There were not many of them. The scale of their activities set them apart from most farmers. For they could have considerable wealth, even in times of great difficulty for cereal growing on the Berkshire Downs, where many of them were based. They also had social standing locally – not on a par with landowners, not even with those whose estates were smaller than the holdings cultivated by these greater farmers – but of considerable degree even so. These farmers could maintain a decent riding stable, might own a carriage, and their

Farmer Hales of Lamport, Northamptonshire, was a man of substance, as his studio pose in the 1860s demonstrates. (Museum of English Rural Life)

womenfolk no longer needed to spend so much time on the work of the farm. All of that earned them the disapprobation of writers such as Richard Jefferies, who regarded farming as needing above all hands-on attention from its practitioners. It could be a closely-knit society. Cornelius Stovin was one of the big farmers at Binbrook, the parish in Lincolnshire mentioned earlier. He was related by marriage to others among the leading farming families of the district – the Riggalls, Sharpleys and Atkinsons. The sons, brothers and nephews of this class of farmer, if they did not go into farming, were likely to enter the professional classes as land agents, lawyers, clergymen.

The farmers with their 'ordinary' farms of one or two hundred acres occupied a place lower down the scale. Not for them a life of riding to hounds, but one of effort from them and their families. Nevertheless, their businesses turned over thousands of pounds a year, and usually earned them enough to live a life of frugal respectability that set them firmly in the middle ranks of village society. They were about on a par with clerks in the towns.

There was a social and economic gulf between the really large-scale farmers and those occupying the smallest acreages. They had in common the name of farmer but not much else. To many nineteenth-century observers the holders of the smallest farms were barely distinguishable from labourers. Indeed, many of them did spring from the ranks of the labourers, taking on a few acres as a part-time holding and, with luck, building up from that to a full-time occupation of something like fifty to 100 acres. As we shall see when turning to the many ways by which the small-scale farmer has been described, these people can be seen as the English peasantry translated into more modern times.

This brings us back to the large number of very small farm holdings: 2,652 of less than fifty acres in Berkshire in the agricultural statistics for 1875. Although recorded as farm holdings, they were not usually reckoned to be full-time occupations. Those who were trying to make a living, from small-scale livestock farming perhaps, would often have a number of these small holdings. Others who had small holdings did not count farming as their principal occupation. They were butchers, perhaps, who had land on which to keep some of their stock; or publicans, coal merchants, and all manner of village society to whom a few acres were useful.

Small farms were to be found throughout the land, but there were a number of areas particularly noted for them. The Fens was a prime example where farming on the small scale was successful on the rich soils. Similar conditions in the Isle of Axholme produced another concentration of small farming. The Vale of Evesham was famed for its fruit growers, most of whom had small acreages. In more general terms, the south-west, the industrial midlands and the north-west were strongholds of small farming in the nineteenth century.

Graziers and cowkeepers

In the occupational tables of the census returns farmers and graziers are usually counted together as one category. It was a reasonable decision because 'grazier' was a term meaning both general and specific. In its general sense it could simply mean a farmer who bought stock for grazing, that is, to fatten them ready for the butcher. They were to be found especially in such districts as the Midlands, where there were rich pastures. There were specialist graziers as well, although not many of them: when separately identified they total no more than 3,000 or so. Some acted more as contractors than farmers, renting land as required, especially those who worked near the towns.

The cowkeeper was quite a different type of farmer: he kept dairy cows. Until the mid-nineteenth century, this was an activity not confined to the village; indeed, it was arguably more common in the towns. In the village, keeping dairy cows was often an activity of the small cottage farmer. He might also be referred to as a dairyman. The transfer of meaning of that word to the seller of milk, cheese and butter rather than the farmer who had the cows followed the development of dairy farming as a recognized branch of commercial farming. An outbreak of cattle plague in the 1860s led to the decline of urban cow-keeping and spurred on the growth of rural dairying, with farmers in such counties as Somerset and Derbyshire supplying milk to the towns by train.

Tenants and owners

Most farmers were tenants – they rented land from another owner of land, most of them private owners, some of them institutions, such as colleges, the church and the crown. The terms on which they held the land varied from time to time and place to place.

The history of land tenure is a complicated one, with various forms of tenure derived from the feudal system lingering into modern times. Feudal land tenure, involving obligations and services due to the lord, broke down in the late Middle Ages. During succeeding centuries most tenurial relationships were converted to monetary value. As will be discussed later, there were remnants of manorial land-holding, in particular copyhold tenure, which continued in existence until finally being abolished in 1925.

Leasehold became the preferred means of letting farmland for many centuries. The sixteenth and seventeenth centuries saw the first big movement by landowners to convert copyhold and other customary tenancies to leasehold, and in subsequent centuries the process continued but was never completed. It was common in earlier centuries to make a grant of tenure for a term of 'lives', usually three. These were the lives of specified people, and at the end of each life, which could mean the actual death of the farmer or a change of circumstances for another reason, the incoming tenant bargained for a new lease of life. Customarily a life was reckoned at seven years, so a lease of three lives meant twenty-one years. Increasingly by the eighteenth century, leases were prescribed for terms of years – seven, fourteen, twenty-one – rather than the 'lives'.

A lease offered the farmer some security of tenure, and the lease of lives an element of family continuity. But by the mid-nineteenth century most farmers held their land on annual tenancy – or tenancy-at-will – rather than a lease of several years. They could, therefore, lose their farms at the end of any year's term. The landlord-tenant relationship did not, in normal circumstances, work like that, and farmers continued in their occupations from year to year, evicted only if they were plainly poor husbandmen, insolvent or of such bad character that the estate could no longer continue their tenancy.

Estate records are a valuable source for tracing farming families, for they are far more plentiful than records of farmers. In the estate rentals and surveys, in tenancy agreements and in letters (though these are less commonly found) it is possible to trace the entry of farming families on to an estate, and the different farms they held.

There were farmers who owned their land. In the nineteenth century about ten per cent of them did so. There were probably more in the seventeenth and eighteenth centuries. The extent to which consolidation of the estates of the gentry and aristocracy brought about a decline in the numbers of independent freeholder-farmers has been a subject of much debate for well over a century. Did, for example, change in agriculture, and especially enclosure, have a major effect, or was it that the bigger estate-owners were in a position to offer good terms to the yeomen? It is a debate that is probably not going to trouble most of us looking for our farming ancestors, except that the influences upon the independent freeholder-farmer, especially those with a small number of acres, can explain why and how some ceased to own their land.

In the twentieth century there was another big shift towards owner-occupation. By 1914 the proportion of farmland owned by its occupiers was already beginning to increase. Some of the vast number of acres George Baylis farmed were his own. On the other side of the landlord-tenant equation, Lord Wantage took the unusual step of farming 10,000 acres of his estate on his own account during the 1890s. Greater change was to come after the First World War, when many estates sold some, sometimes all of their land. Tenants were among the most common purchasers, such that by 1927 more than a third of the agricultural land of England and Wales was owner-occupied.

The farming ladder

It is quite common to hear people say that they 'come from a farming family', the implication being that it has been long-established on the farm, three generations at least. This is a perception of some antiquity. There was a tale told of the Earl of Yarborough, a large landowner in north Lincolnshire, who, when asked how he managed to attract such good farming tenants, declared 'I breed them'. It was something of a chestnut, recounted about several generations of earls, designed to demonstrate the security and continuity of life on the estate. It is certainly true that there was a good deal of continuity, and the Yarborough estate rolls do show a number of farm families who continued on the estate for many years, often from generation to generation.

That is only part of the story, however, for farming society has always been mobile. Reading the 'lifestyle' sections of newspapers today, there are features on old farming families that have been on the same farm for four generations, and others on people who have taken up farming for the first time; and there are those who give up, leaving the farm and perhaps breaking a family tradition. Thus it always has been, and the reasons for these moves are very similar today to those of previous generations. Families may leave the farm through business failure, but as often from there being no one from the next generation to take over; newcomers move in as a change of career, often bringing capital from another activity. There are differences between the ages, of course – former pop stars were not a feature of the farming population in the nineteenth century as they are now, but the principles are little altered.

While some farms have stayed in the same family for generations, many farmers have moved from farm to farm. Some do retire – or, perhaps because farming is one of those occupations from which people tend not to retire entirely, they downsize. Followers of *The Archers* on the radio will recall the way each generation has moved out to pass Brookfield on to the next, while maintaining active interest in the work. In the 1870s Cornelius Stovin retired from the large farm he had held at Binbrook, Lincolnshire, to a smaller place a few miles away. In the opposite direction, a farmer could start his career with a modest farm, and end up with one considerably bigger. Some writers would refer to the 'farming ladder', as though it was an established system rather than the ad hoc movement of farmers enlarging or reducing the size of their farms as circumstances changed.

It was possible, although unusual, for someone to start out as a labourer and end up with a hundred acres or more. There were certain areas of the country where this was most likely to happen. The Fens of eastern England was one of them, where there were more small holdings available on which a labourer might be able to start farming. The Isle of Axholme was another, where it was said at the end of the nineteenth century that several of the largest farmers, with more than 300 acres, had all begun as labourers. Mostly it was the established farmer who moved to a bigger farm, until he reached the time of retiring to a smaller place.

Movement in farming society was likely to increase at times of change and stress in the agricultural economy. Enclosure of the open fields was one of those times. The economic downturns also occasioned increased mobility, forcing some to give up farming, while opportunities were opened up for newcomers with enterprise. There was a recession after the end of the Napoleonic wars, extending for much of the 1820s and 1830s, when many small freeholders seem to have dropped out of farming. In the late nineteenth century, from about 1875–95, there was another downturn, known as the Great Depression. Bankruptcies among farmers increased, and so did the numbers who gave up before insolvency struck; at the same time newcomers were able to pick up farms at very cheap rents. Between the world wars of the twentieth century there was another Great Depression, when the same thing happened again.

Farmers moved every now and again to a different farm; this was often necessary if they wanted a bigger one. Most of them did not move far, usually to another farm on the same estate or in the same general area. It was a common view, not without foundation, that familiarity with local soils and conditions was a considerable advantage. It is relatively easy to trace such short-distance moves through the census, estate papers and county directories. There were not a few farmers who made moves over greater distances, and tracing them might pose some problems. The Great Depression of the 1880s was one period that stimulated such movement, when vacant arable farms in southern and eastern England were often taken up by men from Scotland and the West Country. Some high-profile farmers made the move from Scotland to midland and southern England. Colin Campbell, who was the first president of the National Farmers Union, was a Scotsman who moved to Lincolnshire, while Primrose McConnell, an agricultural journalist, went south to Essex, describing his experiences in *The Diary of a Working Farmer,* published in 1906. Scottish names became common in certain parts of Essex as a result of this movement. These farmers making their long-distance moves introduced the practice of moving their complete farm to their new home, the railway network enabling them to hire trains for the purpose. This went on until the 1950s: a documentary made by British Transport Films told the story of a farmer moving from Yorkshire to Sussex.

Farmers' families

The first people employed on most farms were the farmer's wife and children. For a sizeable minority, they were the only people employed. The general report to the 1851 census noted that a third of all farmers in the country employed no labour. 'Employment' was not really the term to use of family labour for the nineteenth and well into the twentieth century, for wages rarely entered into the equation. Even so, being a farmer's wife was a full-time job, and the same was true for a large number of adult sons and daughters. This was recognized in effect by the nineteenth-century censuses, which had separate entries for farmers' wives and children in the occupational sections. The number of farmers' wives in the census for Lincolnshire was nearly three-quarters the total returned for farmers. It is likely that there were a few more working wives who, for one reason or another, escaped entry in that column of the census. Only the wealthiest of farming families could afford to let the wife withdraw from the business of the farm. To use another slight anachronism, farming marriages for the majority were very much partnerships, and business partnerships at that (the same with most trades, certainly in the pre-industrial period). The importance of the

A farming family: the Wyatts of Cricket St Thomas, Somerset, c1880. (Museum of English Rural Life)

wife's contribution to the management was such that it was unusual for a single man to take a farm. Conversely, the experience gained by the wife meant that it was not uncommon for widows to take on the running of the farm. At each census there were in the region of 570 to 700 female farmers in Lincolnshire. Nearly all of them will have been widows, for social custom and property law militated against a single woman taking a farm on her own account.

Enclosure and the farmer
The eighteenth and nineteenth centuries witnessed a transformation in the farming landscape with enclosure by Act of Parliament of land that had been cultivated in open fields. It was a development that affected many of our rural ancestors, for it involved the redistribution into compact fields of land that they had held in several portions across the parish. There has been considerable debate among historians about just how enclosure affected people, especially the small landed proprietors and yeoman farmers. Did enclosure cause a decline in this class or was a

decline in the number of small proprietors already under way, making it much easier for the smaller number of landowners in the parish to agree on a redistribution of land through enclosure? On the whole the balance has tipped towards the second option in recent decades.

However, what is valuable to the study of family history is that many enclosure documents reveal information about some of the people involved. One of the main series of documents is the enclosure award, which lists the different holders of land and rights in the parish, and their allocation under the enclosure Act. There were maps to accompany the awards.

Berkshire Record Office has carried out a major programme of digitization of the enclosure awards and maps, and the results can be seen on the New Landscapes section of their website.

Yeomen and peasants

'Who were the Yeomen – The Yeomen of England?', ran the opening lines to a song from Edward German's opera *Merrie England*. It was first performed in 1902, when the whole concept of a yeoman seemed to be in decline in the face of large-scale farming. 'The freemen were the yeomen', continued the song, an answer that most of the audience probably knew instinctively was right.

Who, then, were the yeoman farmers? The small-scale and independent farmers, perhaps. That again seems instinctively correct, except that many to whom the term could apply were farming on the large scale. Robert Loder of Berkshire was an example. He was a farmer-landowner in the seventeenth century, and he had a fair amount of land. There were other terms besides 'yeoman' for the really small-scale farmer, to which we shall come shortly.

There was a variety of terms used for those who worked the land in the early modern period. Probate inventories give an indication of this, as a few examples from late-seventeenth century Kent demonstrate. Robert Beane of Hernehill was a 'husbandman'. He left a small estate in 1682 consisting of ten cattle and three pigs, but no sheep. Robert Hilliard was described as a 'yeoman' in 1708. His estate was a little larger: four cows and two calves, two horses, fifteen sheep and thirteen lambs, four acres of wheat, four acres of barley and six acres of oats. Robert Crampe of Hernehill in 1682 left an estate valued £30, including seven milch cows, several other cattle, a sow, ewes and lambs. Crampe, however, was described as a labourer.

Husbandman, yeoman, labourer seem to have been almost interchangeable – distinctions certainly were blurred, but they existed nonetheless. Husbandmen and yeomen were more literate – far more signed their names than those described as labourers. The main differences revolved around title to land. Husbandmen and yeomen usually had some land, and they often owned it as freeholders. They were farming, and the scale of their activities varied. This variation was reflected in the classifications of landowners that distinguished between 'greater yeomen' and 'lesser yeomen' (see below). The labourer was less likely to have any land to his name, and what he had he did not own. What they all had in common was that they were not bound by feudal tenure. Even though feudal tenure had been officially abolished by the 1680s, the descriptions 'husbandman', 'yeoman' and 'labourer' were long-standing indications of free status. These were the freemen of England, as the song has it.

By the nineteenth century 'husbandman' and 'yeoman' were disappearing from common use. Those who classified the different types of landowner might refer to yeomen, but 'farmer' was now the most usual description for anyone who had a claim to working the land, however small the holding might be. George Jones of Kiddington in Oxfordshire described himself in the 1851 census as a 'farmer of 1.5 acres employing no labourers'. A hundred years before that he might have been described as a husbandman, or even a labourer. 'Labourer' by 1851 was used almost exclusively to describe the landless workers. At Ashwell, Hertfordshire, B J Davey records that in the 1830s the farm labourers were said to be 'entirely a rural proletariat', only five out of seventy-two of them having any land to their name.

This change in description had come about partly because there were by most reckonings fewer people who might have been described as yeomen. The number of small freeholders had declined since the late eighteenth century. For a long time it was held that the enclosure of open fields had caused this decline. A classic book by J L and Barbara Hammond, *The Village Labourer*, first published in 1911, was the most popular exponent of this view. It has since been recognized that the process of change was more complicated, and that enclosure did not automatically destroy the livelihood of the small proprietors. Nevertheless, there were fewer of them, and they were generally called farmers by the 1850s.

One historian described the farmers of the smallest scale in mid-nineteenth century Suffolk as 'proprietors of the peasant type', and this raises another issue in describing our rural ancestors. The English have been very proud of not having a peasantry – this was a class that only the continentals had. It has much to do with the association of the word 'peasant' with the servile status of feudalism, and most aspects of feudal tenure declined quite rapidly during the late Middle Ages.

The medieval peasant had been the one who held land by service tenure: in return for the land he cultivated he had to provide service to the lord of the manor. This most often involved work on the lord's land, the demesne farm, but there were other services which could be exacted, such as maintaining the lord's mill. The peasant was higher in status than the serfs or bondmen, who were bound to labour with little or no freedom to change. The peasantry had considerable economic freedom, which enabled some to accumulate quite large holdings of land and wealth to match. At the other end of the scale were peasants who were almost landless.

The break-up of the feudal system resulted in the conversion of almost all the forms of tenure by service into monetary contracts. The term 'peasant' fell out of general currency, as most were keen to emphasize their status as free of servile dues. Those who had a reasonable holding of land became known as yeomen, husbandmen and, later, farmers. Those with little land, as the examples from probate inventories showed, preferred 'labourer' if they could not aspire to 'yeoman'. Later, 'cottager' was a common term. Those with no land were generally called labourers.

Many of those who cultivated the land on the smallest scale could still with justice be described as a peasantry, for they shared many characteristics with their continental brethren. There were occasions when they were indeed so described, as in the Select Committee on Allotments of 1843, which commented on 'discontent ... exhibited amongst the peasantry of the southern counties' in 1830. However, the more common term for such people at this time was 'cottager', and it will be unusual to find our ancestors describing themselves, or being referred to by others, as peasants in archival documents, except perhaps in insulting, ironic or humorous ways. A change came from the late nineteenth century, when a romantic 'cult of the peasant' grew up, elements of which remain in present-day discussion.

Cottagers

A term common in eighteenth and early-nineteenth century literature was 'cottager'. He is one of those people whose position in society was ambivalent, and sometimes further confused by the political ambitions of commentators at the time and later, wanting him to be more than he was in reality. 'Cottager' was generally taken to mean not merely someone who lived in a cottage, but someone who had land, or the right to use land, attached to that dwelling. His land might not be very great – perhaps an allotment of a few perches – but most often amounted to one or two acres. Cottagers were smallholders, and possession of this land was held to give them independence and status.

Cottagers were often desperately poor. Eighteenth and nineteenth-century literature on the plight of the rural poor deals almost as much with cottagers as with the labourers. In many instances cottagers or smallholders were said to be unable to earn as much as a labourer in regular employment. Yet that independence remained paramount, and something to be encouraged. William Cobbett wrote a book on *Cottage Economy*. There were landowners of the early nineteenth century, Lord Carrington and Lord Winchilsea among them, who sought to encourage this sense of independence among the poor by creating cottage or

Mr and Mrs Hall in their cottage home, Gresham, Norfolk, c1860. (Museum of English Rural Life)

allotment tenancies – 'allotment' at this time meaning something considerably larger than today's plot.

Most of the cottagers earned an income from labouring, but some had more independence, described by one mid-nineteenth century writer as 'a kind of farmer themselves, and but a degree below the small farmer yeoman'. They were able to trade in poultry, eggs, livestock and garden crops to earn a respectable sum. Numbers of cottagers were declining by the end of the eighteenth century, and their disappearance was a question much discussed both at the time and since. To many, enclosure was the culprit, depriving the poor cottager of his rights. The Hammonds, in *The Village Labourer*, expressed it thus: 'before enclosure the cottager was a labourer with land, after enclosure he was a labourer without land'. To some extent that was true, as their entitlement to land on enclosure was only very small at best, but, as with most generalizations, it was not the only explanation for the problems of small-scale farming.

From the middle of the nineteenth century, mention of 'cottagers' declined in discussion among contemporaries. 'Cottager' as a description does not entirely disappear. Flora Thompson refers to cottagers, and in the county directory for Herefordshire in 1937 there is a couple of pages of entries for 'cottage farmers'. However, a new term was entering the debate, the smallholder.

Smallholders

Peasant, husbandman, yeoman, cottager – the descriptions of people with small numbers of acres which they farmed either full time or along with some other occupation have changed through the ages. Smallholder is the latest of these, a term that became more common during the second half of the nineteenth century. It is worth noting here that if you have seen a modern translation of Domesday Book it probably refers to the smallholders of a manor. The Latin words are *bordarii* and *cotarii*, which scholars always anglicized as bordars and cottars. These were people with small amounts of land, so translators now prefer the modern terminology of smallholders.

Estate records begin to refer to smallholding rather than cottage tenancies round about the middle of the nineteenth century, and bundles of smallholding tenancy agreements survive in a number of archive collections. It was a political campaign for land reform that really brought the question of the smallholder to greater prominence and established the term in the language. Campaigners such as Jesse Collings and Henry

George wanted to create a new class of small proprietors: 'three acres and a cow' was one of their slogans. They did not achieve all they wanted, but they did get new legislation passed in the form of two Smallholdings Acts of 1892 and 1908, which gave powers to county councils to buy and set aside land to let as smallholdings. Those of our ancestors who leased such land were very likely to be described, and to describe themselves, as smallholders.

Their forebears before the mid-nineteenth century, however, were more likely to be called cottagers, or small yeomen, or even simply farmers, depending upon their status in the locality and the size of holding they had. In the northern counties of England the small farmers were called 'statesmen'. Or they were known by the trade they had alongside working the land, for many small parcels of land were occupied by butchers, innkeepers, dealers, and other tradesmen.

Gardeners and nurserymen

The production of vegetables and fruit on small holdings of land is an age-old part of agriculture, what would be referred to now as market gardening. That is a relatively new term. It was not until 1911 that the census included 'market gardener' as an occupational category, although the term had been entering general currency for some time before that. Going back to the mid-nineteenth century and earlier, the specialist grower of horticultural crops was most usually referred to as simply a gardener, and the census used this as an occupational category during the nineteenth century, sometimes adding 'not domestic' to make clear who was to be included. Nurserymen and seedsmen were added to this category from 1871 onwards.

The land which the gardener occupied was, naturally enough, a garden – or garden ground, as many eighteenth and early-nineteenth century writers would call it. Cottagers, on their smallholdings, would also be growers of horticultural crops, something encouraged by writers as a means of alleviating poverty.

Sources for farmers

Besides the census, the records of births, marriages and deaths, and directories, the main source of information about the farmers is the estate and its archives. Most farmers were tenants, and records about their tenancies were created and held by the landlords. Among these may be found rentals and tenancy agreements, which show what farm the tenant held, its size and the rent paid for it. A good run of these can show when farmers came and went from the estate, and any changes, such as a move to another farm, or the enlargement or reduction in size of the farm rented. The estate records might in addition have maps showing the precise location and extent of farms, and correspondence files.

Not all farmers were tenants, of course, and for these property records – title deeds, sales records – and land tax records can provide basic information. Other sources that record the farmer and his farm are the tithe and enclosure records. As we go further back into the time of customary tenancies the manorial records also become useful sources, in which the entry of a farmer on the court roll is made.

Farmers did create some of their own records, including diaries, accounts, employment and wages books. They were, however, notoriously poor at record-keeping: agricultural journals of the nineteenth century regularly contain articles exhorting farmers to be more business-like in their record-keeping. Commercial stationers

A nineteenth-century farmhouse in Berkshire. (Author's collection)

produced account books suitable for farmers. Most, however, if they kept records at all, seem to have settled, if not for the back of an envelope, then a pocket book or similar, which was easily destroyed. The survival of farm accounts as a result is very small as a percentage of the number of farmers.

Farmers have been subject to government scrutiny, mainly since the mid-nineteenth century. Evidence has been collected from them for parliamentary enquiries and royal commissions, often citing the names of the farmers. These are published in the Parliamentary Papers series. Statistics have been collected from farmers, but the returns from individuals are not usually available. A number of records are available from the Second World War, however. Survival of papers from the county war agricultural executive committees is patchy, but a major project, the National Farm Survey of 1941–43, did generate a lot of useful records about farms and their occupiers, including maps. They are all kept at The National Archives.

Chapter 4

THE ARISTOCRACY AND GENTRY: THE RURAL LANDOWNERS

A recent survey has reckoned that a large proportion of the population can claim descent from the aristocracy. Of course, that is unlikely to give us any claim to titles or estates, the English system of promogeniture (inheritance through the eldest son) ensuring that the descent that most can trace will be through collateral and cadet branches of families. David Hey's book *The Oxford Guide to Family History* includes a photograph of the Duchess of Abercorn in about 1900 together with more than a hundred of her immediate descendants, ably demonstrating the ramifications of such a family. The inter-relationships within landed society are complex. Henrietta, Countess of Oxford and Mortimer in the mid-eighteenth century, referred to all the Cavendishes, Holles, Pierponts and Harleys to whom she was related. This prompts serious consideration of who the aristocracy, the gentry, the landowners in rural society were.

The aristocracy and gentry were the people at the top of the social tree in the conventional divisions of rural society. They were relatively few in number, just how many depending on how inclusive one was in counting. They owned land, or at least the heads of the families did, and those landowners were small in number. In the mid-nineteenth century interest in who owned the land grew; a number of books were published, such as *The Great Governing Families of England* by J L Sanford and M Townsend in 1865, and in 1873 an official survey, the *Return of Owners of Land*, popularly known as the 'New Domesday', was produced. This revealed that about 2,250 people owned about half the enclosed land in England and Wales.

The landowning class was not homogeneous any more than others were. Indeed, they were not thought of as a class so much as a 'landed interest', which gave a different outlook to rural society. There was a broad distinction between the aristocracy, who had titles, and the gentry, who did not, and again between greater and lesser gentry. These distinctions were also based mainly upon the size of the estate and the income derived from it, on which the landowner's social prestige and political influence depended. The aristocracy by this reckoning had the greater estates: broadly speaking, they were the owners of at least 10,000 acres and income of £10,000 per year. The 1873 return listed 363 owners of estates this large: 186 of them were peers, fifty-eight baronets, and 117 untitled. There was thus some blurring in the definitions, if a peerage was the qualification for membership of the aristocracy. The Chaplin family in Lincolnshire was one of those untitled owners of many acres, 20,000 of them, far more than many peers, especially those of recent creation, who might have no more than 3,000 acres.

There was a certain amount of fluidity within aristocratic society which could enable Henry Chaplin to mingle freely with marquesses and princes, and allow younger sons and brothers to be included, along with the holders of Irish titles such as Lord Palmerston. In the appropriate circles, however, the precedence of rank and title was strictly observed.

Many of the owners of very large estates held large tracts of the northern and western counties; land here was often of poor agricultural quality. Conversely, the home counties were more crowded with smaller estates, as landowners of all types sought a base near the capital. Some aristocrats with mainly northern estates had land nearer to London, such as the Duke of Northumberland at Syon Park.

If there was fluidity within the ranks of the aristocracy, there was even more within gentry society. These were the commoners who owned estates of lesser status, which in the nineteenth century were usually taken to be those between 1,000 and 10,000 acres. Some authorities then divided this group further into the greater gentry, who had more than 3,000 acres, and the squires with 1,000–3,000 acres. In 1873 there were about 3,000 people who fell into the category of gentry. There was room within this society for newcomers who had made money in the professions, the military, political service or trade, to move into landed estate. They might buy land or acquire it through marriage. This movement was happening at least from late-medieval times, and continued in the nineteenth and twentieth centuries as cotton-masters, brewers and publishers all aspired to country life. Some very large family estates could originate in this way. The foundation of the Sykes estate at Sledmere, Yorkshire, in the eighteenth century was through wealth derived from the trade of Hull.

The term 'gentry' is of relatively recent origin, arising mainly from the mid-nineteenth century studies of landed society. Before then 'gentleman' was the term more likely to be used, and documents will add 'gent.' after the name of someone with that status. The term 'esquire' might also be used. Originally the esquire was an attendant to the knight at arms (his shield-bearer, specifically). Later it was applied to younger sons of noblemen, and by the nineteenth century was being used more widely for a landed gentleman. Indeed, greater farmers were starting to adopt the style early in the nineteenth century, leading to accusations that they were aping their social betters. However, they had some justification in that, where there was no resident landlord, the main farmers assumed social leadership of the village. 'Esquire' soon slipped further down the social scale to middling farmers and professional men. White's *Directory of Lincolnshire* for 1856 declared that it used the term sparingly 'to avoid invidious distinctions', but it was fighting a losing battle, as 'esquire' lost all specific meaning, being applied to anyone who seemed respectable. The shortened form of the word, 'squire', is a looser term, but tends to refer to the landowner who was resident in the village, as opposed to the one who lived miles away, and most often a member of the gentry rather than aristocracy.

There was much discussion as to what constituted a gentleman. Basically, a gentleman required an income from land or government stock to support suitable leisure and status. He might well have a farm, but his livelihood did not depend upon it; conversely, a working farmer could not be described as a gentleman. Patrick Colquhoun, a social statistician writing in 1801, described this class as 'gentlemen and ladies living on incomes', and he numbered 20,000 in this category.

In the social hierarchy of landownership, the yeomen came below the gentry. These were the proprietors of land on the smaller scale, to whom reference has already been made in chapter 3. J Bateman, who wrote one of the leading books of the nineteenth century on the landowners, divided the group into greater and lesser yeomen and small proprietors, giving an air of precision to what was in reality a very fluid term in common usage. It could be applied to the larger tenant farmer as much as the owner-occupier farmer. Sir Charles Blois in the eighteenth century let his house, Grundisburgh Hall in Suffolk, to a 'yeoman'. Basically, 'yeoman' implied a status above the general run of working farmer. Quite often, tradesmen who bought land would call themselves yeomen, the first rung in the social ladder towards entering the gentry. Yeomen were

The frustrations of the family historian's life: no one seems to know who this gentleman is, except that he is a Somersetshire squire round about 1895. If he is your ancestor, let me know. (Museum of English Rural Life)

of a high status in parish society; they were reasonably well off. They were the ones who were likely to put some money into local improvement, such as the turnpike trust or the local branch railway line. The capital for the Charing turnpike trust in Kent, for example, came almost entirely from people described as yeomen and gentlemen.

The structure of landownership underwent considerable change in the late seventeenth century and first half of the eighteenth. A new governing class following the restoration settlement began to build up its estates. They did this through marriage alliances which brought them land through inheritance, and by buying land from gentry families who had run out of heirs. The Walpoles and the Foxes were two families that increased both in status and landed wealth during this period.

The landowner and rural society
The landowner had an assured place in village society, but the intimacy of his connection with the working life of the parish might be limited, conducted at one remove through the estate agent. Even the resident squire was not necessarily closely involved with his parish. Charles Gray Round was an Essex squire of the mid-nineteenth century. His life was built around his public service on the quarter sessions, the Board of Guardians, the committee for the lunatic asylum and other work. He served as MP for a term. In his immediate locality he supported the parish church and its school, and other local charities.

Sources for landowners
Landowners being at the top of the social tree, one might expect a respectable quantity of records about them, and to a considerable extent that is true. Much has already been recorded about the lineage of many landowning families for the purposes of proving descent and title to land, grants of arms and general family prestige. The College of Arms in London can, therefore, be a useful place for research to establish what genealogies have already been produced which might offer leads into your family tree. The heraldry itself can prove an interesting line of approach.

The management of large estates and households could generate a considerable volume of documents. Their rate of survival is quite high and can go back many centuries, some as far as the medieval period. The first port of call, therefore, in studying the history of landed families is the archives of the estate and family themselves.

Estate papers are concerned with the land and its management. They do not necessarily provide a great deal of information about the family that owns the estate. In fact they might say more about others – the tenants, the people with whom the estate traded, the people involved in transactions for acquiring or disposing of land. The survival of estate correspondence, however, can yield something about the relationship of the landlord to his tenant.

Family and household papers have more to say about the landowners and their families. These might include household accounts, correspondence and diaries. The wide-ranging connections of landed society were such that these sources can provide useful information about more than one family. Some of these documents have been published. A well-known late-medieval collection is the correspondence of the Paston family in Norfolk. They were first published in the late nineteenth century, and there have been several editions since, the most recent edited by Norman Davis in 2004. There are also some transcripts of the letters available on the internet.

There is a considerable literature on the landowning families. There are histories of individual families, usually written by a member of the family, and including genealogical tables. Roger North's *The Lives of the Norths*, published in 1890 about the North family, earls of Guilford, is one literary example. Standard reference works, such as *The Complete Peerage*, Burke's *Peerage* and *Landed Gentry*, provide good background information on families, while nineteenth-century directories record the main owners of the parishes and their seats. To those can be added the work of more recent historians of landed society.

Despite such a wealth of sources, they do not cover every family of landowners. More than one aristocrat has made the observation that the survival of the records of his family can be put down to their happening not to move house in 500 years. However, most families are subject to more movement than that. Even some of the greatest landed families of past centuries have died out, moved away or disposed of their houses, and with them have often gone their records. When it comes to the smaller owners, the gentry families who sold their estates in the twentieth century, the volume of estate and family papers is often diminished. All is not entirely lost, however. Sometimes the records of these families are subsumed into those of others to whom the house passed, while the public nature of the landowning life has meant that monuments, memorials in church and other records often survive from a family long since gone from the village.

Chapter 5

THE GREAT HOUSE AND ESTATE

T he landed estate and the 'big house' employed a large number of people in various capacities. There were grooms and coachmen, carpenters and gardeners; indoors there were butlers, maids and kitchen staff. It was common for the landowner to have charge of the outdoor establishment, while his wife managed the household and its accounts.

At the head of the estate's administration was the steward or the agent. The estate needed efficient management if its owner was to reap the benefits and make the contribution to national and local politics and society that was expected of him. Some landowners handled their own estate administration, but most, even those who took an intimate interest in the workings of their estate, employed some assistance. Nearly all employed an officer who had been known since the Middle Ages as the steward. His functions hardly changed between the thirteenth and the eighteenth centuries, and nor did the methods by which his accounts were presented. In the late eighteenth century things began to change. Landowners such as Thomas Coke, the great landowner at Holkham in Norfolk, were investing in improvements to their estates, and, to administer the changes to the management of the leases and tenancies, employed modernizing stewards who adopted newer accounting practices and record-keeping. Thomas Coke found such a steward in Francis Blaikie. Among the outcomes of this process was an increase in the salaries paid to the stewards, from about £300 a year in 1790 to £500 a year by 1810. Another was that the estate steward increasingly became known as the agent.

The men who took up these positions were often from gentry or farming families. Francis Blaikie was an example of the latter; he was from a Scottish farming family, another fairly common feature of the new breed of estate managers. Indeed, it was common enough to attract the attention of William Cobbett, who did not approve, and to merit a reference by Jane Austen, who in *Emma* included the remark that

'Mr Graham intends to have a Scotch bailiff for his new estate'. The estate owner's family was another common source of agents. Hon. Edward Strutt was the brother of Lord Rayleigh, who became the manager of the family estates in Essex in the nineteenth century. Another common route into estate agency was from the legal practice, while a few agents had previously been local tradesmen or clergymen. Some family dynasties became established in the world of estate agency, among them the Wyatt family in Staffordshire, and the Strutts, for out of Edward's work for his brother grew the independent estate agency business of Strutt & Parker.

Only the largest estates had their full-time resident steward or agent. Most landowners employed the services of independent professionals who served other estates besides theirs. Before the rise of the independent estate agency, it was the local solicitors or surveyors based in the market town to whom the landowner turned to manage the estate and collect the rents. Records of country solicitors and estate agents can thus provide information about farming and estate families.

Below the agent was often a number of local agents or bailiffs. This was especially necessary on the large estates, spread over several parishes or even counties; there would be a local resident agent, while the main estate administration might be elsewhere.

The gamekeeper gained something of an elite status in landed society as the popularity of the shoot grew from the mid-eighteenth century onwards. In 1853 there were 1452 licensed keepers, a relatively small number as not every landowner indulged in the expensive practice of nurturing his game. The gamekeeper was not always the most popular of people in the countryside: the farmers did not care for having their crops eaten by protected birds and rabbits, while other villagers wanted free access to the wild game.

The census for 1851 recorded eighteen indoor servants at Sledmere, the home of Sir Tatton Sykes, one of the richest landowners in the East Riding of Yorkshire. They included a cook-housekeeper, governesses for the children, a maid for Lady Sykes, the butler and footmen. James Best had thirteen servants at his house, Boxley in Kent, in the 1750s: a butler, groom, coachman, postilion, gardener, housekeeper, cook, nurse and five maids. These examples were typical of the size of household establishment, between one and two dozen servants, that was common amongst the greater gentry and aristocracy of the eighteenth and nineteenth centuries. The grander houses had a larger complement. At Badminton, Gloucestershire, at the end of the seventeenth century the

Duchess of Beaufort was said to have a household establishment as large as 200. That was rare, but other great houses might have forty or fifty servants. At the opposite end of the scale, smaller estates could afford only a modest household, but could often manage at least a cook, a few maids and a groom and gardener. The smaller the household, the more versatile the servants had to be, the footman having to attend to the garden, for example.

There was a strict hierarchy amongst the household servants: the butlers, cooks, housekeepers and ladies' maids were far superior beings to the footmen, grooms and maids. In the greater households the different classes of servant had little to do with each other. The butler had responsibility for the footmen, the housekeeper for the housemaids and laundry maids, and

Estate gardeners at Sulham House, Berkshire, 1884. (Museum of English Rural Life)

the cook for the kitchen maids, scullery maid and dairymaid. The lower ranks tended to be local and were likely to stay for a relatively short time, leaving often when they married to set up home. There were more career butlers, cooks and housekeepers, and they moved about the country far more. Disagreement with the lady of the house, especially when a new one took over, could be the occasion for their leaving a position. To get a new senior servant of quality required some effort, and, once found, such a one was worth keeping: P G Wodehouse used the qualities of Anatole the chef to good effect in his tales of Jeeves and Wooster. Family grapevines were useful means of finding staff: when Lady Sykes wanted a new housekeeper, her sister-in-law recommended someone from London.

Sources for estate families

Until recent times the people who worked in the big house and on the estate were most unlikely to leave any record of their activities. Twentieth-century oral history projects have recorded some accounts, and a few of those who worked for landed families have written of their lives. Among the most numerous first-hand accounts have been those of gamekeepers, for the sporting life has engendered its own literature. Publication of such books grew from the late-nineteenth century onwards. John Wilkins published *The autobiography of an English gamekeeper* in 1892, for example, and it was reprinted in the 1970s. A steady flow of such memoirs has followed, such as this example selected almost at random: Thomas Isaac, *The wind in my face: a gamekeeper's memories*, published in 1966. More unusual are the Norfolk gamekeeper's diaries of the early nineteenth century published as *The Banville diaries: journals of a Norfolk gamekeeper, 1822–44*, in 1986.

There were instruction manuals for household servants, such as *The Compleat Servant* by Samuel and Sarah Adams, published in 1806. Most of the information about the estate and household workers, however, will come from the records of the families who employed them. They may be recorded in accounts, diaries and correspondence, especially the more senior staff, those who stayed with the family a long time, and those with a special place in the house, such as nannies and governesses.

Many workers in the great households gathered memorabilia of their time and their employers. Collecting family crests, cut out of envelopes, was one little hobby amongst butlers and footmen. The albums in which these were kept and other items of memorabilia might survive amongst our family effects or in museum collections.

Chapter 6

VILLAGE TRADESMEN AND BUSINESSMEN

The village tradesman can be no less elusive than the other inhabitants of the countryside. I mentioned in the introduction that my grandfather was a country baker before the Second World War. His was a small-scale operation. He did not have a shop. He started off baking cakes in the cottage range in his kitchen before progressing to a bakehouse in his garden – a very large shed, really. He baked his bread and cakes and cycled round to deliver them (often it was my father and his brother doing the rounds). He had no entry in the directories. He probably did not think it worth while, having built up his round by word of mouth. Presumably he made some records of his business transactions, but he certainly did not keep them. His activities as a baker have really disappeared without trace, apart, that is, from the scales and some loaf tins. He stopped trading in the Second World War, and answered the call for temporary help at the Post Office. He worked for them until he retired. There will be many more like him – small, independent traders, who would take up other occupations from time to time.

This points us to some important reminders when using the county directories. They are invaluable: apart from the census, they are often the only source for information about tradesmen in a nineteenth-century village, but they are not always complete or up to date, any more than their equivalents are today. The directories are as accurate as the information given to them, and there are many reasons for things to go wrong, at least from the historical researcher's point of view. Some people did not have an entry. Businesses might have to pay, so not all bothered; they had their trade without this particular means of promotion. There were people working for one dealer who would not merit an entry – the women in the villages around Luton plaiting straw for hats, for example. Using directories to date businesses is never an exact science. Some took an entry some time after they had started in business; conversely, some still had an entry after they had ceased trading. Seasonal trades are often under-represented, their practitioners perhaps being under another heading or not at all.

Descriptions of tradesmen are variable, something that both directories and census returns reflect faithfully. The father of John Constable the artist is sometimes described as a miller. In fact he was the owner of one or two mills rather than the man who ground the flour. But someone described as a miller might, like Constable, have been the owner of a mill, the tenant who worked the mill or the hired hand, for the word might be used in all three senses. And during the course of his career a man might move through all three of those descriptions.

Directories were first published at the end of the eighteenth century. Before then the major source that can give us information about the village tradesmen is the probate inventory. The accounts of gentry households and estates can also indicate the people with whom they dealt.

The range of businesses in the village – the tradesmen, craftsmen and those involved in industrial work – was wide, embracing aspects of manufacture, retail and services. Distinctions between these were often blurred, as such tradesmen as the saddler, the shoemaker and the basket-maker made the goods they sold on their premises. The trades were continually changing: by the beginning of the twentieth century, trades connected with cycling and motoring were joining those working with horses, for example. It will not be possible to represent the whole in this short essay. The tradesmen were not found everywhere: one of the marks distinguishing the small hamlet from the village was the presence of tradesmen. But the village did not have to be very large to support at least some trades. A population of 350 or so would be enough for a publican to make at least a part-time living in the first half of the nineteenth century, and 450–500 was sufficient to introduce some of the craftsmen. Not every village had a tradesman of each type, and the composition of businesses in any one village can seem eclectic as we look at the directories. But the range of businesses that could be found in even a moderate settlement could be considerable. Much depended on the locality. The small village of Sand Hutton in the North Riding of Yorkshire, with a population of 275 in the 1830s, is only three miles from the market town of Thirsk, but communications were sufficiently difficult for it to have three shoemakers, four publicans, two shopkeepers, a butcher, a baker, and a tailor. Even in 1900, the population little changed, there was still a shop, butcher, blacksmith and, a new trade, cycle agent. The large village of Binbrook has been introduced already: its remoteness in the Lincolnshire Wolds helped keep fifteen shoemakers, eighteen dressmakers, thirteen tailors, thirteen blacksmiths, fourteen wheelwrights, five butchers, and seven millers in work in 1851 working for the village and its fairly extensive hinterland.

Most rural trades and industries were small-scale, one-man or family businesses. Large numbers combined more than one trade. Most joint occupations were related in some way: the butchers who were also cattle dealers; the wheelwright and joiner; the draper and tailor. But there were others with a much looser connection. Coal merchants took on quite a range of different trades – corn dealer and carrier, for example. There was a village in south Cardiganshire where the publican at the Carpenter's Arms was a carpenter; he also had a small farm. Many tradesmen had some land. Often it was accommodation land for the carrier's horse or the butcher's grazing land, but farming on the small scale was common among tradesmen, so common that most did not bother to mention it in directories. A few managed quite a range of trades. George Ramsey in the north-Lincolnshire village of Roxby was described in the directory for 1851 as a bricklayer, mason and grocer; he also had the local post office.

Many rural trades and crafts went into decline during the late nineteenth century. They were often unable to compete with the cheap products of industry. The country saddler, for example, was undercut by the products of factories in the Midlands. If their trade was only with the immediate neighbourhood of the village, there were fewer customers, because the village population had gone down. The tradesman was probably better off based in the market town, able to pick up trade from a wider area. The classic book, *The Wheelwright's Shop* by George Sturt, is about one such business, based in the Surrey market town of Farnham.

Country crafts have shown remarkable powers of resilience, however. Trades such as thatcher, blacksmith and farrier and potter continued throughout the twentieth century. They adapted to satisfy new markets such that by the end of the century some were showing new signs of growth.

Rural crafts or rural industries

When we think of rural trade and business we usually think first of the crafts that have just been mentioned. We don't think of the brewery, the foundry, or even the quarry and mine. However, all could be found in the villages of England and Wales at various times in the past. Indeed, most of the early stages of the Industrial Revolution were located in rural areas.

The first cotton mills were nearly all water-powered and thus sited where a mill could draw power from the rivers and streams. Pennine valleys and the Peak District of Derbyshire were among places in which new cotton and woollen mills of the eighteenth century were built. The growth of the industry often turned villages into towns; even so there were many textile mills that were still essentially village undertakings in the twentieth century, such as the woollen mills of the West Country and Wales. Detail on workers in the textile industry is really beyond the scope of this book: there is a companion volume, *Tracing Your Textile Ancestors* by Vivien Teasdale (Pen and Sword, 2009).

Mining and quarrying, too, must be excluded, but it is worth remembering that at times these activities could bring some of our ancestors into relatively remote spots. Rosedale Abbey in North Yorkshire today has about 300 people living in it, about what it had in the mid-nineteenth century; it bustles with the walkers and other holiday-makers. But between the 1850s and 1920s the mining of magnetic iron ore brought an influx of people, quadrupling the population.

Among the new industries that came to the countryside during the nineteenth century were the makers of agricultural implements,

Workers at the village foundry at Bucklebury, 1890. Most of the names of these men and boys are known. (Museum of English Rural Life)

producing the new tools that farmers were using. Directories were recording them by the 1830s. Most were based in market towns, but there were not a few in the villages. In Lincolnshire there was a machine maker at the village of Burton on Stather, a substantial village which had a population of about 700 in the 1830s. There was a foundry in the village of Bucklebury, Berkshire. James Smyth started making seed drills in the Suffolk village of Peasenhall in about 1800, and by the 1830s the factory was producing 200–300 of these machines each year. Despite not being on the railway line, his business stayed in the village and prospered. Compared with bigger, urban industries, this was a small operation, with seventy employees in the 1870s. In the village that made it a major employer – some of those recorded as labourer in the census in this parish were working in the factory rather than on the farm.

Some rural businesses did grow. There were rural entrepreneurs who built up strong enterprises. The Fisons fertilizer company was one. The Fison family in Norfolk had wide-ranging business interests, including malting and milling, dealing in coal, manures and fertilizers. Theirs was something of a mini-conglomerate spread across rural East Anglia and employing quite a few people.

The wheelwright

Springtime was the busiest season of the year for the village wheelwright. It was then that the farmers discovered or remembered all the faults in their implements which needed to be put right before spring cultivation could get under way. Down they came to the wheelwright's shop with the wagons with broken spokes and rotting side boards, the seed drills with broken shafts, even the small tools such as forks in need of a new handle.

The wheelwright did not just make wheels – or even carts and wagons (the distinction between the two was that the cart had two wheels, the wagon four). He had a much wider range as a craftsman in wood serving the village. Wheels he would often have to make new – the wagons regularly needed new ones – and a complex, time-consuming job it was. But he might not often get a chance to make a cart or wagon from scratch. His brethren in the town with bigger workshops tended to do more of that. Besides, a new wagon would set the farmer back £30 or more, so it was not one of his regular purchases – as long as he could bring it creaking along for repair, he would do so.

There had been two related trades, cartwright and wainwright, which survive in surnames. By the eighteenth century distinctions between them and the wheelwright were breaking down. Quite why it was that wheelwright became the common term while the others fell out of general usage is not clear. He was one of the most common tradesmen in rural England and Wales. The 28,000 recorded in the census for 1851 included those working in the towns, some being employees of larger engineering concerns; it is those town-based men who probably accounted for most of the increase in numbers in successive censuses until 1871. Even so, the trade of the rural wheelwright was slow to decline during the late nineteenth century. There was considerable overlap between the wheelwright and the blacksmith, especially in the nineteenth century, when wheels were more usually bound with hooped iron tyres which had to be shrunk on to the wooden wheel. Many combined the trades of wheelwright and blacksmith. Some wheelwrights also extended their range of skills into those of millwrighting, the

The wheelwright at Fawley, Herefordshire, 1937. (Museum of English Rural Life)

maintenance of the wooden gearing in windmills and watermills. At the other end of the scale of skills there was overlap with the general carpenter, and some were described as wheelwright and carpenter.

The blacksmith

One of the more common tradesmen in the village was the blacksmith. His connection with farming was of the closest, there being such steady demand for his services in shoeing horses, repairing implements and other metal work that he could be based in the village as much as the town.

Bucklebury in Berkshire was a small village, but it had enough trade to keep a smith busy and it was here in the mid-eighteenth century that John Hedges was the smith. His family had been smiths there for 150 years, and succeeding generations were to continue the business for another 150, turning it into the foundry business mentioned earlier. John Hedges' accounts survive, and from these we can see that almost all of his customers were farmers. They came to him with their horses to be shod and their ploughs to be repaired. Time and again they brought their ploughshares and coulters to be reshaped, sharpened and repointed. These, the cutting blades of the plough, were costly to buy new in 1750, so it was worth while for the farmer to keep them going a few years by having them sharpened at 10d a time.

Shoeing horses and sharpening shares accounted for almost half of Hedges' work. Then there were all the other farm tools to be repaired – the spades, rakes, forks and billhooks were all brought in for attention. None was too small to repair – even the bolts and pins holding tools together were considered worth the repair, so high was the cost of iron then. Putting tyres on wagons was a bigger job, and fairly regular work.

As well as work for farmers, John Hedges had domestic goods to repair. He mended Lady Long's 'coffey pot' and her apple roaster, and sharpened her scissors. He mended Rev. Annesley's bedstead, cheese toaster and his 'chockalit pot'. These were well-to-do clients: the poor cottagers most likely had their pots and pans mended by an itinerant tinker who charged less.

Times changed, and so did the work of the blacksmith. By the mid-nineteenth century ploughs had self-sharpening shares, so John Hedges' successors had little work repairing them. They were not mending spades and shovels so often, either, but instead keeping the array of bigger implements – scarifiers, harrows, mowers, threshing machines –

Extract from the day book of J B Packer, blacksmith at Uffington, Berkshire, 1897.
(Museum of English Rural Life)

that farmers now had in good repair. And there was still plenty of work shoeing horses. This adaptability kept blacksmiths busy well into the twentieth century, some as shoeing smiths, some as manufacturers of decorative ironwork, while other smiths' businesses were transformed into garages and repairers of motor vehicles.

Carpenters and builders

Carpenters and joiners were common among the village tradesmen. These were general workers in wood, not necessarily particularly skilled. They undertook building repairs, made coffins, fences, furniture. They might graduate into the realms of the wheelwright and millwright, for which greater skill was needed.

Building trades were also fairly common, including some general tradesmen, and more specialized workers, such as thatchers and slaters. Most builders in the villages worked in a small-scale way, but some did develop firms of some local substance in the late nineteenth and twentieth centuries.

Millers

The miller was a common feature of village society until the large mills at ports took away most of his business from the late-nineteenth century onwards. The flexibility of language is such that 'miller' in different contexts might refer to someone who owns the mill, the one who operates it or the employees.

The rural mill ground the grain of the locality for bread and for animal feed, and most parishes contained at least one mill. Their sites were determined by the supply of power – along the stream for the watermill, up a hill for the windmill. Milling had been a manorial monopoly during the Middle Ages. There was often only one mill for the manor, to which all tenants had to bring their grain. With the break-down of the feudal system a different hierarchy developed. Some mills had a wide commercial trade, serving the major towns. These were big mills, sited on the rivers that offered good transport out to the markets. The millers were in full-time business, whereas those with small country mills, serving their locality only, often combined the milling with another business. Farming was a common combination with milling; publican was another.

Shops and retailers

The village shop has quite a long pedigree, but it has vied with itinerant sellers for the custom of the country dweller. Indeed the itinerants were almost certainly in the majority in the seventeenth and eighteenth centuries. They went from village to village driving carts, riding ponies or simply walking, carrying their wares for sale. These were the 'chapmen', a term that originally referred specifically to the travelling seller of books and magazines (known as 'chap books') but had widened to refer to almost any itinerant tradesman. There were chapwomen as well. Elizabeth Lawrence of Donington-on-Bain, Lincolnshire, was one. When she died in 1670, her stock-in-trade listed with her will consisted of a small number of pins, needles, buttons, cotton, tape, laces and combs. Dorothy Wordsworth recorded in her diary for 1800 that 'the Cockermouth traveller came with thread, hardware, mustard, etc. She is very healthy; has travelled over the mountains these thirty years'. This woman always walked: her husband had declared that the ass she wanted would be demeaning for a respectable tradeswoman.

By the eighteenth century these travelling salesmen were known more often as tallymen, pedlars, cheapjacks (or cheap johns) and hawkers. 'Huckster' was another term often used for country dealers, but it also might have disreputable overtones. In official terms, 'pedlar' and 'hawker' were the preferred terms: from 1697 'pedlars and hawkers' licences were required by itinerant street traders, and when the census started recording occupations in greater detail in 1831 such traders were all called hawkers. In other usage, hawker referred more often to the door-to-door seller of urban areas, less often to his rural counterpart, for whom the term 'pedlar' was more usual. This urban influence probably lay behind much of the increase in the numbers of hawkers recorded in the census, from 9,457 males in 1831 to 11,099 in 1851. The number of women hawkers increased even more: between 1841, when they were first recorded, and 1851 numbers went from 3,563 to 9,230. Some of this might have been due to under-recording in the first census, but there was undoubtedly increasing trade for these people.

A high proportion of the itinerant tradesmen were based in the towns rather than the villages. They bought their goods at the fairs and travelled out from the town round the surrounding villages, often covering vast distances. That was by no means universal. Barrow-on-Humber, a large village with a population of more than 2,000 in 1851, and had been home to James Pilkington, a traveller of the early seventeenth century. He died in 1635, leaving a substantial estate worth £242. Some of the profits from his retailing had been invested in farming, for he held twenty-one acres of land at his death. His was an unusually successful business; most travellers did not aspire to such wealth. At the other end of the scale were the poor traders such as the two described by William Cobbett in his *Rural Rides*: 'two lazy looking fellows, in long great coats and bundles in their hands ... vagabonds of this description are seen all over the country with tea licences in their pockets. They vend tea, drugs and religious tracts'. He evidently did not approve of them.

Probate inventories from the late sixteenth century show an increase in the number of retailers with settled businesses. Most were in market towns, but certainly by 1600 the first village shopkeepers can be identified. Two of these early shops were found in South Creake in Norfolk and Botesdale in Suffolk, and there were a few more in Gloucestershire. By the late seventeenth century shops were not at all uncommon in villages, although the claim of a pamphleteer of 1680 that 'in every country village where is (it may be) not above ten houses, there is a shopkeeper' was a wild exaggeration. Wills and inventories of the late seventeenth century mention drapers (dealers in woollen and linen cloth), mercers (dealers in silk goods), ironmongers and the occasional grocer amongst village tradesmen. The grocer, strictly, was a wholesaler, but closer study of the inventories shows that already the distinctions were blurring. Stephen Alvery of Kirton in Holland, Lincolnshire, was a mercer who died in 1685. His inventory is that of a more general retailer, with a good stock of groceries, ironmongery and books.

A mercer in a village might seem a bit high-class, but that was the nature of trade for most rural retailers in the eighteenth century. They supplied the needs of the upper ranks of society – the labouring classes bought from the itinerants. It was not until the nineteenth century and the coming of the railway that the village shop became a place that catered for everybody, and even then there were distinct social gradations between different shops. Most of them were described as grocer and draper, but others were known simply as shopkeepers. Villages were able to support a remarkable number of these. Legbourn, a village of 551 inhabitants in 1851, had, according to the directory of the time, three shopkeepers, in addition to George Aram, the tailor and draper. Such people ranged in scale from the successor of the eighteenth-century mercer, who had most of the gentry trade, down to the widow selling a few sweets from her front room.

Besides the shops and itinerant sellers, there were various dealers and traders in the countryside who bought and sold on behalf of the farmers and their wives. Some came out from the town, but others were based in the village, often people with a small amount of land who engaged in a bit of dealing as well. One particular trader of the countryside was the higgler, who dealt in poultry and eggs. He, or sometimes she, would travel round the farms collecting produce to take into market.

The village of Kilburn, north Yorkshire, where once there were four shoemakers. The main village industry now is the workshop of Thompson's 'Mouseman' furniture. (The author)

Shoemakers

At the beginning of the twentieth century Mr Goodricke, a resident of the north Yorkshire village of Kilburn, died. He had been a cobbler, as his grandson told the registrar when he went to register the death. The registrar paused, raised his eyebrows, and turned to his clerk: 'Put boot and shoe repairer', he said. Shoemaker or cobbler, he was one of the prominent village tradesmen. Outdoor work and unmetalled roads were enough to keep him busy – and his fellows, for there was often more than one shoemaker in the village. Kilburn is a small village, but in the 1890s there were three others besides Mr Goodricke in business as shoemakers. By this time mechanization in the shoe trade was having its effect – new sales were more often of ready-made boots, leaving the village cobbler with the repair work. In the end this was to be the undoing of him, and it was rare to find a shoe-mender in the mid-twentieth century village.

Butchers and bakers

The Lincolnshire village of Binbrook, referred to earlier, had five butchers in the census of 1851. Only four of them were entered in the directory, which suggests that the last one was in a small way of business. This was

Outside Mr Ing's butcher's shop, Haddenham, Buckinghamshire, about 1900. (Museum of English Rural Life)

a large village, evidently able to support so many. Numbers of butchers were more or less pro rata with size of population: a village of 500–600 had two or three, below that size they were uncommon. The butcher's trade, therefore, came from his home village and from the smaller villages in the locality. He sold mainly to the upper sections of society – the labourers and cottagers were too poor to eat butcher's meat very often.

Entries in census returns and directories suggest that most butchers were full-time. Some, however, were recorded as having other trades, especially farmer or grazier; publican was another not uncommon additional occupation. Some were involved in a little dealing. Many had small landholdings – records of their holdings appear in estate archives, for example – most often a field or two on which to keep their stock-in-trade.

'How shameful for a labourer's wife to go to the baker's shop', complained William Cobbett in *Cottage Economy*. It was a growing trend, yet bakers were far less numerous than butchers, certainly as far as being entered as a main occupation in the census or directories was concerned. Binbrook, with its population of more than a thousand, apparently had none, and many another large village was similarly ill-provided. The village baker, however, did not have the certainty of business from gentry and middle-class residents, who either had bread from their own cooks or dealt with market-town bakers. That left the village to people like my grandfather, who do not appear in the directories.

Transport services

According to the 1831 census there were 12,835 carriers, and this total had risen to 25,834 in 1841 and 43,710 in 1851. A growing economy needed more people to transport its goods, and although most of this increase will have been in urban transport, workers in these services were also to be found in the countryside.

The country carrier's business was in taking goods and people from village to market town, and back again. He was at the bottom of a hierarchy of road transport services: at the top were those engaged in long-distance trunk services between major towns and cities; below them were regional carriers; and then came the local carriers. Country carriers were widely distributed, some based in the market town, but many were in the village, their routes being mainly home-and-back journeys to the town.

Much of the trunk carrier's trade was taken by the railways during the nineteenth century, but for the country carrier the second half of the century was something of an Indian summer. The number of regular services from the villages on market days – most were recorded in the county directories, with the name of the carrier – was increasing rather than declining. The carrier would pick up his passengers around the villages, together with the goods people wanted to be taken in, and shopping lists, for some carriers would undertake errands on the villager's behalf. It was an unhurried journey: Arthur Randell, in his book *Sixty Years a Fenman*, recalled the seven miles from the village of Magdalen to King's Lynn in Norfolk taking about three hours, arriving at the town about mid-day. The return journey started at about three o'clock in the afternoon. That pace meant that about fifteen miles distance from the town was the maximum that carriers would cover.

The drovers were specialized transport contractors, who took cattle and sheep from their breeding grounds to the grazing fields of midland England, and on to the markets around London. Men from Scotland brought cattle down through the Pennines to south Lincolnshire and Norfolk, and from Wales drovers were responsible for transporting cattle from the western Welsh counties to the English midlands. There were

A country carrier and his van. (Museum of English Rural Life)

English drovers as well, some engaged in long-distance trade, for example from Norfolk and Northamptonshire where cattle were fattened to the markets around London. Even geese were marched up from Norfolk for London's Christmas markets. The traffic was extensive, and at times it seems as though there was a regular procession of animals along some of the main roads. In the early 1830s about 182,000 sheep and 26,000 cattle were travelling the roads between south Lincolnshire and London each year, managed by eighty-six drovers.

Besides these drovers, there were others undertaking more local business, although they might not always appear described as such, as they probably had other strings to their bow. Under the vagrancy laws introduced by the Tudors, drovers had to be licensed to prove that they were in legitimate trade. A licence was issued only to men over thirty who were householders, and married.

Many, probably most drovers engaged in the long-distance trade were independent dealers, and were men of some substance, for they needed capital to fund their trade and their journeys. They were also entrusted with considerable sums of money on behalf of the farmers and tradesmen with whom they dealt. The organization this required meant that they were likely to keep records of their transactions, and a number of drovers' accounts do survive, which provide information both about the drover and some of those with whom he dealt. Out of these business connections, some drovers were involved in the foundation of banks: most famously, David Jones, a Welsh farmer's son, founded the bank that was to become Lloyd's from his droving activities.

The census started recording drovers as an independent occupation in 1841, when there were 2,058 in England and Wales, rising to 2,970 in 1851. The expansion of the railway network led to their decline during the second half of the century.

That expanding railway network brought new opportunities to the countryside, providing work for many who left agriculture but did not want to leave the village. In the first place there was the work of building the railway line. Many of those who worked for the contractors came in

Railway workers loading parcels on a train for Skegness at Firsby junction in 1946. The young man whose attention was diverted by the camera was called K Smith. (Author's collection)

from outside and then moved on, but there could be some local recruitment. Once finished, the railway needed porters, booking office clerks, signalmen, crossing keepers and others. Apart from the station master, whose career could take him far from home, many of the staff at the country station were drawn from the locality, such employment being a big step up from farm labouring. Figures for country employees of the railways are hard to come by, but they could be quite substantial. My grandfather the baker's village station was a busy junction which had more than a dozen staff, taking into account the shifts that had to be covered. Even a small wayside station might account for five or six people – one of the reasons why branch lines had difficulty paying their way.

Sources for rural trades

At the beginning of this chapter I commented that rural tradesmen can be elusive, and so they can. Their names and mention of their trade can be found in the principal sources, such as the census returns, parish registers, probate records, directories and manorial court records. There are several ways in which these can be inaccurate. One is that we have to rely on self-description, or perhaps the description provided by the census enumerator. Sometimes people might overstate or understate what they do, depending how they want officialdom to view them. Sometimes people can be simply vague; this might seem odd until we recall the times when we are not sure how to describe our occupations when the official database offers a range of options which do not quite fit.

There can be under-recording of multiple occupations: the publican, perhaps, does not see fit to mention that he also engages in cattle dealing. There can be changes in occupation recorded from one document to another, and we need to distinguish between those which arise from looseness in description and genuine changes; and it is not always straightforward. Someone might appear in one document as a carpenter, in another as a wheelwright. This might be because he began working as a youth as a carpenter before gaining the skills of a wheelwright, or buying the local wheelwright's business; or it might be because descriptions are applied in a vague fashion. The chronology of documents may help answer such questions.

Records created by the tradesmen themselves are few, even from the larger village businesses. Not many ledgers, day books or letter books from village blacksmiths, country builders or shops survive. There are some, but if we are looking for particular traders and their families, the disappointments might well outnumber the successes. There are more the closer we get to our own times, but even then they are not numerous – of the thousands of village shops and pubs that have closed in the last thirty or so years, how many have sent records to the archive offices?

Often it is the more ephemeral items that do survive – letterheads, business cards, bills. If the business was large enough to print publicity material, leaflets and catalogues can also survive. Some of these might turn up in our own family papers, but they can equally appear amongst the papers of those with whom the tradesman dealt. It might be worth looking in estate and farm records, therefore. Unfortunately, for this type of document to be individually listed requires cataloguing in detail greater than record offices can afford.

Interest in watermills and windmills has been considerable for a century or more, with the result that much local information about them has been gathered. There are local publications and the volumes of the

Tradesmen's receipts can provide information from their letterheads. This, bundle preserved on its spike, is from Wilshire. (Museum of English Rural Life)

Victoria County History can provide information. The Mills Archive Trust is a good place to start a search for ancestors who were millers. It has built up extensive collections of material on individual mills and millers, and holds the millers and millwrights database. The trust is based at Watlington House, 44 Watlington Street, Reading RG1 4RJ, its website www.millsarchive.com. Its collections are open by appointment.

The records of the more industrial undertakings are just as variable in their survival. The business archives of Smyth of Peasenhall do survive, however, held in the Suffolk Record Office, Ipswich. There is a catalogue online: www.suffolk.gov.uk/LeisureAndCulture/LocalHistoryAndHeritage/Suffolk RecordOffice/. The records of the firm's employees are not among those to survive, however.

One should not forget the importance of things, of objects. Those scales I've mentioned before and a few baking tins are all that survive of my grandfather's time as a baker in his village, and this makes them of some family-historical value. Many of us perhaps have chests of tools that were used by a grandfather for his trade, and if he was the second or third generation in that trade, some of the tools might be of some antiquity. If that is so, it is worth making a record, for as our society uses less oral transmission of its past, it is not possible to rely on saying 'it was handed down'. And if at some point the objects are offered to a museum, that provenance becomes important. All of this means that museums as well as record offices can be worthwhile places for study as we seek out the context of our ancestors' trades.

Chapter 7

VILLAGE SOCIETY

Rural clergy

The parish clergyman had an ambivalent status in the village. He was often of gentle birth: the church was a common occupation for the younger sons of the landed classes. Most parsons, however, came from more humble backgrounds, and the education they gained in going into the church could represent social advancement. The clergyman was perhaps the most learned man in his country parish, and as such accorded respect. Many noted literary figures, from Gilbert White, Jane Austen and Lord Tennyson to Rev W Awdry, have their connections with the country parsonage. In other respects, however, he lacked the attributes of a gentleman, most importantly land and wealth.

Until parliamentary enclosure and later reforms to the tithe, the parson's income was derived almost entirely from tithes, and there was considerable variation between rich and poor. Tithes in medieval times had been divided into 'greater' tithes, which were paid to the rector, and the 'lesser' tithes paid to the vicar. Often the abbot of a monastery held the rectory, which had been assigned to his house by some benefactor. Unable to perform the parish duties himself, the abbot appointed a substitute, the vicar, creating a differentiation in the naming of parish 'livings', as they were known, that has held to this day. The Reformation transferred the rectories to the landowners who acquired the monastic lands, giving them rights to appoint parish clergy.

Some clergy had a small amount of land – the glebe – attached to their living. The process of enclosure often allocated additional land, creating the Rectory Farms to be found in many parishes. Some did very well out of this: in two parishes in Oxfordshire the cleric held more than 1,000 acres. Most had far less, but having this land to their name raised the status of the rectors and vicars who held it to something akin to minor gentry. There were some clerics who were landowners in their own right, either by inheritance or by purchase. 'Squarson' was the term coined to describe those who combined roles of squire and vicar. These men with the land and the richer livings were the rectors and vicars who were appointed as magistrates in increasing numbers. In some places – Bedfordshire was one – more than 40 per cent of the county bench was made up of parsons. At the same time this movement widened the gulf between the rich clergy and poor, between those with livings and the curates.

The richest livings in the eighteenth century could be worth as much as £400 a year. They were few, however, and mostly in the gift of the greater landowners, to whose sons they almost always went. Most country livings had very poor incomes, less than £100 a year in the eighteenth century, and often £50 or less. Many clergymen held more than one parish simply in order to build up a respectable income. The curates, who had to carry out many parish duties on behalf of the vicar or rector, were paid far less – as little as £5 a year. Their material lives were little better than the labourers of the parish among whom they worked. Reforms during the nineteenth century attempted to even out differences in income, but most country livings remained poor. Indeed, a link was made between stipends and the price of wheat, which made matters worse in the late nineteenth century when prices fell considerably.

It is small wonder, then, that the poorer clergy had to turn to other occupations to help make ends meet. They were often the schoolmasters of the parish: before village schools became more common they would take pupils into their homes. This was the stuff of many a novel: for example, the education of Tom Tulliver in *The Mill on the Floss* by George Eliot. The building of parish schools in increasing numbers from the 1830s onwards drew the parson in as contributor to the teaching. He was also involved with the welfare of the parish, with the established charities, and with the new institutions of the state, regularly being a member of the Boards of Guardians.

While the clergy of the established church enjoyed some status in the village, if little wealth, the non-conformist ministers had neither income nor status. The same could be said of Roman Catholic priests, who had to live a shadowy existence until the emancipation of the nineteenth century allowed the church to set up a parish structure again. Before that the priests who worked in the countryside were almost all private chaplains to aristocratic and gentry families who had never forsaken the 'old religion' during the Reformation.

The incumbents in the rural parishes of England and Wales are generally well-documented. A visit to the church will sometimes find them listed in a chart on the wall or in the local church history booklet.

Quarterly meeting of the Bude Methodist circuit, Cornwall on 24 June 1909, the first one to which women were admitted. (Museum of English Rural Life)

Documentation is to be found in the diocesan records, and two publications of the nineteenth century provide information about incumbents. A number of editions of *The Clerical Guide and Ecclesiastical Directory* were published from 1817 onwards, and *Crockford's Clerical Directory* was first published in 1858, and has been issued regularly ever since.

The Methodist church in its various branches (Wesleyan, Primitive, and so on) was organized into 'circuits', a group of churches centred on the local market town. Their quarterly preaching plans setting out which minister or lay preacher was to conduct the worship at each chapel survive to varying extents, mostly in the county record offices.

The professions
Most of the middle-class professional people were based in the market towns. The offices of the solicitor and the surveyor were most likely to be found there. Their connections with village society were closer than that, however, for many had land and lived in the village. Christopher Comyns Parker and his son Oxley Parker were surveyors and tithe surveyors, but they were also landowners in Essex. Their family became

the Parker of the estate agents and surveyors Strutt & Parker, and their extensive family and business papers in the Essex County Record Office are a valuable source for farming life between the 1820s and 1880s. John Omer was a surveyor in Norfolk in the late eighteenth century who also farmed as tenant of the Holkham estate. The firm of Cluttons had its origins in a country surveying business in Sussex.

Parliamentary enclosure in the eighteenth century produced another group of professionals and semi-professionals in the enclosure commissioners. Some made almost a full-time occupation out of this work, surveying a large number of parish enclosures, but most were less fully committed. While surveyors were prominent, enclosure commissioners were drawn from a wide range; some were urban men, others lived in the countryside. Among them were farmers such as Philip Skipworth from north Lincolnshire and James Florance from west Sussex; there were many clergymen, and the occasional tradesman, such as Thomas Taylor, who was a carpenter of Swanbourne. The large numbers of enclosure awards, maps and other documents that survive record something of the lives of ancestors who worked in this way.

Other members of the professional classes resident in villages could include doctors, solicitors and surveyors. They were more likely to be found in the large villages. Binbrook in Lincolnshire, certainly within this category, numbered among its residents in 1851 two doctors, an architect, a solicitor and a surveyor. However, smaller villages could be home to a few such professional families in the eighteenth and nineteenth centuries. By the end of the nineteenth century and into the twentieth some new professional services might be found among the village residents – veterinary surgeons, for example – and the arrival of the motor car meant that some began to choose the village for home while working in the town.

Private residents – the middle class of the village

The county directories published in the nineteenth century regularly had a section in the entries for each parish headed 'private residents'. These were the people who had an independent income, and were thus to be separated from the farmers and tradesmen who worked. Some had connections with landed families but owned little, if any, themselves. Amongst them might be found retired military men, professional people who wanted a house in the village rather than the town, and single ladies.

These people often lived in 'villas', a term adopted in English originally to describe a mansion in the Palladian style, but by the end of the eighteenth century appropriated for the more modest detached houses on a good plot of two to ten acres on the edge of the village. Later still, 'villa' descended the social scale to become the term for large detached and semi-detached Victorian Gothic houses built in the suburbs of such towns as Oxford, the homes of the professional classes.

The new services

From the late eighteenth century onwards a range of new services penetrated the countryside: post office, road construction, schools, water and electricity, and so on. Many were not entirely new, of course. The parish had always had its overseer of the highways, for example, who

Not the village policeman, this man was a special constable in Herefordshire. He did not even get a uniform, just an armband, when he was on duty on the occasion of a visit by Queen Mary in the 1930s. (Museum of English Rural Life)

organized road maintenance. However, the eighteenth century introduced a new element with the rebuilding of roads under the aegis of the turnpike trusts. Most of the trusts were locally based, and trustees included local landowners and some of the greater farmers. Later, the

Sutton & Sons, the seedsmen, set up this photograph of the village postman delivering their seeds in the 1890s. (Museum of English Rural Life)

new local authorities established in the nineteenth century assumed responsibility for the highway, and the contractors maintaining the roads became a common feature of rural life.

Order in the village had been maintained by elected parish officials, such as the constable. Nineteenth-century reforms introduced professional police forces. The Cheshire Police Act 1829 created the first rural police force, and other counties followed suit, especially after the County Police Act 1839 enabled county forces to be established without separate legislation for each one. Within two years of that Act twenty-four police forces had been founded. Most were still small in scale, but by 1851 Lancashire, the largest, had a complement of 509. Soon the police house became a feature of many villages.

Along with the railway, the police force was an attractive route for advancement for agricultural labourers. The prospects and pension were considerable inducements to join the force. In turn, the police found in the agricultural workers a good, dependable source of new constables, who in many places provided the main part of the rural constabulary.

When Laura left Lark Rise she went to work at the Post Office, another new feature of rural life, whose development followed the introduction of the penny post in the 1840s. The village post office was usually in one of the shops, while the postman became a character of the village.

Village schools

Bradfield in Berkshire is nowadays a school with a village attached. This independent secondary school is now large, with 700 pupils. There are a number of similar examples of big schools in rural settings, where schoolmaster will be a fairly common occupation. When we think of village schools, however, the image is usually of the much smaller institutions with a few teachers, the type of place Gervase Phinn used to inspect.

What Bradfield College has in common with the small village primary school is that, founded in 1850, it dates from the time when education in villages was expanding, and we can expect to find ancestors involved in it. The Church of England, through its National Society, had since the early nineteenth century been making a concerted effort to make up for deficiencies in educational provision, and the school is one of the characteristic buildings added to the village. Non-conformist denominations were doing the same through the British and Foreign Schools Society. Added to the independent day schools,

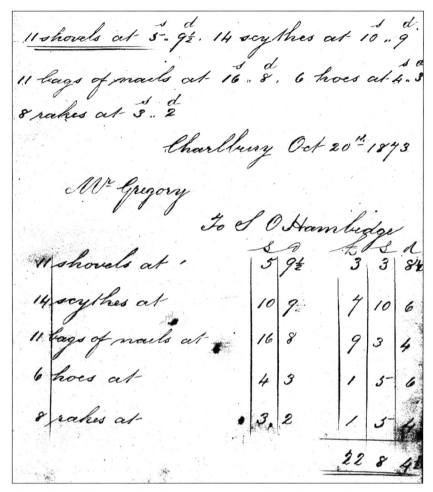

Master S Hambidge kept this school exercise book in 1873. This page of exercises shows the concerns of rural education of the time. (Museum of English Rural Life)

endowed village schools, dame schools and others, educational provision in the village was well established by the time the Education Act 1870 introduced new state elementary schools.

Even though most of these developments post-date the introduction of the census, tracing the teachers is not always straightforward, as many were part time, and not always recorded as such. Other sources include school records; where they survive, they are usually in local record offices. Episcopal visitation returns often comment on schooling, and HM Inspectorate of Schools was established under the provisions for state funding of 1839. Inspectors' reports are in The National Archives.

Village organizations

Village charities
Many village charities were founded after the Reformation to take the place of the monasteries in supporting the poor and sick. Churchwardens' accounts give a wealth of information on the way they were run.

Some seventeenth-century churchwardens' accounts have been transcribed and published. Many, however, remain in manuscript form, and one needs to be able to tackle early-modern handwriting, with its variety of abbreviations.

Benefit societies
Mutual benefit societies to support people in adversity and old age first appeared in Scotland in the late seventeenth century. They spread throughout the kingdom during the next hundred years, and grew in number. An Act to regulate them was passed in 1793, and 5117 local friendly societies were registered. Sir Frederick Eden argued that unregistered societies brought the total to more than 7000. This figure included societies in industrial towns, but there were already many small clubs in villages, attracting very loyal support. In 1818 the first county friendly society was formed in Essex, followed by similar societies in Hampshire (1825), Kent and Wiltshire (both 1828). They all worked in a similar way: for an entrance fee and a regular monthly subscription, a member was entitled to subsistence in sickness and his widow to a payment on his death.

Many of these societies were fiercely independent, restricting their membership to their locality; others during the nineteenth century became affiliated and in time incorporated within the larger groupings, such as the Manchester Unity of Oddfellows. The societies were often not benefit clubs only, but a source of friendship and conviviality – their meetings were usually at a pub. A more sober feature was their annual parade through the village, ending perhaps with a church service.

Among the nineteenth century's popular activities for cottage-dwellers was the keeping of pigs. Many landowners and farmers encouraged this as a means of greater self-sufficiency for the poor. A pig could provide a

RULES & ORDERS

FOR THE GOVERNMENT OF THE

Benefit Society,

ENTITLED

'The Red, White & Blue,'

HELD AT THE

Bull Inn, Filkins.

~~~~~~~~~

Established May, 1879.

~~~~~~~~~

Oxford:

PRINTED AT THE HOLYWELL PRESS,

1907

The title page of the rule book of the Red, White & Blue Benefit Society of Filkins, Oxfordshire. (Museum of English Rural Life)

year or more's supply of meat, but the cottager had to wait a year or so before the pig was ready for slaughter. To help with building up funds for the purchase of a pig, pig clubs sprang up, into which a small weekly subscription was paid.

The village band leading members of Meare Friendly Society, Somerset, on their parade through the village in about 1910. (Museum of English Rural Life)

This is Garsington village cricket team, not posed in their whites, but setting out in the charabanc for an away match in about 1900. (Museum of English Rural Life)

Recreation

Village life had its times for relaxation, and since the mid-nineteenth century this has created village hall committees, village players, cricket clubs, annual flower shows and the like. The active among our forebears might feature in reports of these activities, in programmes, newspapers, even committee minute books. Some of the societies that furthered these activities are of some age: gardening and floral societies can be found from the late eighteenth century. Allotment clubs to promote self-sufficiency amongst labourers date from about the same time.

The survival of records is variable, for they are essentially ephemeral – even the committee minutes are likely to have been treated as such by the volunteer members. These are the type of documents that turn up in our own family 'papers', someone else's family, or scattered amongst record office collections. It is difficult to find a structure for searching for them, which adds to the fun when something turns up. Little will predate the mid-nineteenth century, as most recreational activities before then lacked committees and programmes.

Chapter 8

RURAL MIGRANTS AND THE RURAL POOR

Rural society included a lot of people who moved in and out of different occupations, and often moved from place to place to do them. Many were among the casual and itinerant workers already mentioned in chapter 2. There were the visiting workers from outside, among them the migrant Irish harvest labourers, such a feature of nineteenth-century farming. Most of these men returned home regularly at the end of the harvest season, but there were some who stayed on, perhaps marrying a girl they had met on the way. They were not the only ones taking such work, and English villagers would go on the tramp taking on casual harvest work.

There were many seasonal occupations that people took up from time to time. Brick-making was one: William Maynard in Sussex was a brick-maker in summer and a hoop-shaver in winter. Suffolk labourers regularly travelled to Burton upon Trent to work in the maltings during the winter. George Ewart Evans, a pioneer in oral history, made a classic study of this migration. Such studies as this, and unpublished collections of oral history, are the main sources available for finding out about rural ancestors who joined the migrant workers.

Romany and gypsy people were among the migrants. The Romany and Traveller Family History Society has a guide to some of the basics of tracing Romany ancestors (www.rtfhs.org.uk).

Evacuees

During the Second World War many thousands of children were taken from the towns to safer havens in the countryside. It was a formative period of life for many, traumatic for some. A collection of archives, arising out of research at the University of Reading, has been gathered at the Museum of English Rural Life. It includes letters and oral history, but not all of the collection has yet been catalogued.

The poor

Measuring the extent of poverty is never an exact science, and many of our rural ancestors could be counted among the poorer members of society. The wages of the farm labourers of southern England in the early nineteenth century, less than 10 shillings a week, afforded little more than subsistence living. Independent cottagers were often no better off. This had been recognized by Gregory King when he compiled his population statistics in 1688; he counted cottagers in with paupers and vagrants to make a group totalling nearly a quarter of the population.

For the most part, however, 'the poor' is meant those who need support beyond what they earned, and most of those at one time or another came into the range of official oversight. In tracing them, therefore, it is useful to know the structure of administration of poor relief – the poor laws. This is not the place to go into detail – there are other books that do that, such as the companion to this one by Robert Burlison, *Tracing Your Pauper Ancestors*, but a little explanation will help here.

A key piece of legislation was the Act for the Relief of the Poor 1601. Tudor governments had tackled the question of how to deal with the destitute and vagrants following the closure of the monasteries, and this Act was the culmination, establishing the basis of poor relief for the next two centuries. It had four main bases: the provision of almshouses for

Memorandum from a notebook kept by Joseph Shakell, who was a landowner and overseer of the poor in Buckinghamshire in the 1830s, during the transition from the Old Poor Law to the New. (Museum of English Rural Life)

those unable to work, the old, sick or disabled; provision of work for the able-bodied; supporting apprenticeships for the young; punishment of the idle – the beggars and vagabonds, who could be whipped and sent out of the parish. Administration of the poor law was in the hands of each parish, and parish overseers had considerable freedom in its interpretation.

The Act of Settlement 1662 established the grounds on which entitlement to parish relief could be claimed. Besides being born in the parish these were the payment of rent on a property, apprenticeship in the parish, and working there for a certain term. This could be for no more than twelve months, giving rise to some contracts for farm servants being for fifty-one weeks, to ensure that no right of settlement was established. Paupers unable to show their right of settlement could be sent away from the parish, officially to their place of settlement, but overseers might content themselves with depositing the pauper in a neighbouring parish.

Many amendments to this system of poor relief were made during the next two centuries. In the eighteenth century parishes were enabled to join together in 'unions' to build a joint workhouse, for example. But the basic structure held good until the end of the eighteenth century, when the growth in population, the effects of industrialization, and the stresses from the wars with France began to make themselves felt in rising poor rates. In the rural areas, the farmers, on whom the burden of rates mostly fell, complained, and general concern about the working of the poor laws resulted in a new system established by the Poor Law Amendment Act 1834. This New Poor Law, brought into effect in 1835, abolished relief through the parishes and with that the office of parish overseer. In its place the unions of parishes were made universal and placed under the local supervision of boards of poor law guardians.

A characteristic feature of the New Poor Law was the workhouse. It was not a new institution, but now every poor law union was expected to have at least one, and it was to be run on the principle that life in the workhouse for the able-bodied would be less attractive than gainful work outside. There were many ways in which the administration of that regime was made less harsh; nevertheless the indignities of the workhouse achieved notoriety, in particular the segregation of sexes that involved the separation of family members. These things remained in memory long after the last structure of the New Poor Law was finally abolished in 1948. The poor law unions were mostly based around market towns; the workhouse was also sited there, which meant that the poor of the village moved to town if they entered the institution.

Administration of the poor laws created its bureaucracies, and they in turn created documents in quantity, many though by no means all of which survive. Because of the survival of such official records the poorest in rural society are sometimes better documented than many others.

There are printed sources, such as the annual reports of the Poor Law Commissioners and enquiries into the working of the laws published in the Parliamentary Papers. By far the most detailed was the Poor Law Commission of 1832, from which the Poor Law Amendment Act followed. If you are searching for specific people, or even specific places, such official publications might not be a major source, although they do cite examples. After 1834 the manuscript sources are the records of the boards of guardians. These include minute books, registers of births and deaths, and the workhouse registers of admission and discharge, which record name, place of birth, occupation and church affiliation of the paupers. There might also be registers of offences, records relating to medical condition and records of children boarded out from the workhouse.

The county record offices hold most of the guardians' records, and The National Archives has the records of the national Poor Law Commissioners responsible for maintaining the standards throughout the country. Amongst the national records are registers of the officials employed by the guardians, including the relieving officers, masters and matrons of the workhouse. If you are searching for someone from a particular parish, nineteenth-century directories say which poor law union that parish is in. There are internet references which provide guides to the poor law unions, such as www.institutions.org.uk.

Records of the Old Poor Law from the seventeenth century (especially from 1660) to 1835 are also reasonably plentiful. The main series are the records of the parish overseers and vestry, principally the minutes and accounts. There are also collections of overseers' correspondence in many record offices. These include letters written by or for individuals seeking relief of some kind. They are a rich and valuable source for the study of the poor and the administration of relief before the New Poor Law of 1834. They are also voluminous, which means that there is not generally a quick, indexed route to find records relating to individuals. However, scholars are working on the records, and some letters have been published, for example, Thomas Sokoll, *Essex Pauper Letters, 1731–1837* (2001).

Some other poor law and settlement records have been published, mainly by county record societies, and a few are available online, such as the database compiled by the Sussex Record Society (www.sussexrecord society.org.uk).

The working of the Act of Settlement was also administered by the overseers and the vestry (for the vestry see the entry in chapter 9). Among these documents are settlement examinations, which are often quite detailed records of the labouring classes, as the overseers carefully recorded all the evidence to justify someone staying in the parish. Amongst the information recorded can be details of occupation including work history, places in which the applicant has lived, his family and any property he has rented. Certificates were also given to a worker going to a job in another parish acknowledging the parish's responsibility towards him should he become destitute. Removal orders issued against those not having legal settlement in the parish likewise provide information on occupations and the parish to which they were to be sent. Concern to ensure that fathers took responsibility for their children often made bastardy examinations detailed accounts. The overseer applied to a magistrate for an order to be served on the parents, and the mother was examined by the magistrate to establish the circumstances. Apprenticeship records can also be rich in detail.

The quarter sessions provide another layer in the administration of the poor law. It was a meeting of the quarter sessions in Berkshire in 1795 that made one of the most famous changes to the administration of the poor law by instituting payment of allowances in aid of wages to working labourers, something that became known as the Speenhamland system after the village in which the magistrates met. Poor law matters coming before the magistrates were often the disputed cases, and the sessions had to issue orders to the parish on settlement and removal.

Sir Frederick Eden's book *The State of the Poor,* published in 1797, was one of the most detailed contemporary accounts of the workings of the poor law. The final volume cited numerous cases; he identified individuals only by initials, but they might be enough to aid some family searches.

Chapter 9

SOME RECORDS
AND SOURCES

In this chapter some of the major classes of archival and printed sources are described, with notes on how they can be used and where to find them. They are in alphabetical order, although this does mean that there is a bit of overlap between entries.

Births, marriages and deaths

In 1538 Thomas Cromwell instructed the rectors and vicars of every parish in England and Wales to make records of baptisms, marriages and deaths. These, the parish registers, are among the basic tools for the family historian. In 1837 civil registration was introduced, but the new records do not immediately supersede the usefulness of the parish registers.

Like most records, they are not always easy to use and not absolutely perfect for the purposes for which we might want to use them. Not many registers go back as far as 1538, and series of registers are often broken during the sixteenth and seventeenth centuries. The period of the civil war and Commonwealth is a particularly difficult one: records were either lost or not properly kept up. Early registers are often in Latin; even in English some of the handwriting is not easy to decipher.

Baptismal registers in particular are prone to omissions and estimates. Some children were not baptised until some time after their birth, giving rise to entries describing a child as 'about two years old'. Some who died in infancy did not get registered at all, and we may never know about them. Some non-conformists were not registered, although their numbers were not great, as most Quakers and other dissenters were content to go through the rites of the Church of England.

Marriages are not always easy to identify because of the frequency with which people found partners from outside their parish. A radius of about ten miles accounted for most. Marriages solemnized after the calling of banns were registered in the parish, but marriage by licence –

the stuff of many a novel – was common, allowing the couple to be married outside their home parishes. These were recorded in diocesan registers but not always the parish. A well-known example is the marriage of William Shakespeare and Anne Hathaway, which was by licence issued by the diocese of Worcester.

An Act of Parliament of 1753 attempted to regularize the recording of marriages to prevent clandestine marriages, of which there had been many. Further standardization came in 1812, when printed forms were adopted. These included information which hitherto had often been omitted, such as the occupation of the father in baptismal registers.

The registers were kept in the church, in the parish chest, and for centuries that is where they remained. Long after the establishment of county record offices many were retained by the parishes. For accessibility and ease of use, that meant family historians often had to use the 'Bishop's transcripts' – copies of registers made for the diocese. These were deposited in the diocesan record office (the county record office or other major office was granted this role) and the family researcher needs to know which diocese the parish was in historically. The Bishop's transcripts are prone to error, and do not always include the full record. Serious efforts were made in the late twentieth century to get the original parish registers deposited with record offices, and very few now remain in the parish.

Not everyone was a member of the Church of England – indeed, non-conformity has been strong in village society. While many accepted Anglican rites for births, marriages and deaths, the dissenting churches did maintain their own registers. Those of the Quakers reach back to the mid-seventeenth century; for other denominations the starting date for registers is usually the eighteenth century. For all, the best place to search is The National Archives, where duplicate sets of registers were deposited. Roman Catholicism has not been quite so strong in rural areas, except amongst the recusant of the gentry class. In general they went along with Anglican practice for registration.

When civil registration was introduced, copies were kept locally at the office at which the birth, marriage or death was registered and at the General Register Office, which used to be based at Somerset House in London. The present General Register Office can supply copies of certificates:

Certificate Services Section, General Register Office, PO Box 2, Southport, Lancashire PR8 2JD. Telephone 0845 603 7788. www.ips.gov.uk.

Indexes to registers of births, marriages and deaths are available in many local libraries and record offices, usually as microfilm. There are many online sources for indexes, and some transcriptions of registers. Some are free, such as www.freebmd.org.uk and www.freereg.org.uk; others are pay-to-view. A good starting point is the National Archives website, which provides links to other useful sources (www.nationalarchives.gov.uk).

Census returns

The census returns are among the most basic tools for the family historian. Together with parish registers they enable us to start creating a family tree, to discover family connections, to find where our ancestors lived and something of what they did.

The United Kingdom conducted its first population census in 1801, and censuses have been held every ten years since then until, it seems, 2011. There was one exception to the series, when the census due in 1941 was passed over because of the Second World War. The first censuses were very basic and did not record the names of everybody, although some included the name of the head of the household. In 1841 the full record of names and ages of each member of the household was gathered for the first time. From 1851 the censuses become more useful, as more information was collected about such matters as occupations and place of birth, enabling us to gain more basic knowledge about our forebears of the nineteenth century.

The results of the census are published shortly afterwards in summary form, giving details for country, county and borough. The full records are not made public until 100 years after the census. The most recent to be released is the 1911 census. The complete records can be seen by visiting the National Archives. In addition many local studies libraries and record offices have copies of census returns for their district, usually on microfilm.

There are websites that make available census records from 1841 onwards. The simplest way to find them is through the National Archives' website (www.nationalarchives.gov.uk). Most of these are pay-to-use sites (not all make this very clear on their home page), but the 1881 census can be seen free at www.freebmd.org.uk.

Church records

As well as the parish registers of births, marriages and deaths, there are records about the church itself. There is a wide range of these, from minutes of meetings to magazines and locally produced histories of the church. All can yield information about our ancestors who were involved with the church. Those who held an office will be recorded, and this can extend beyond the roles of churchwarden, elder, steward and deacon to organist, Sunday school teacher and flower arranger.

Most surviving local church records are held in the county record offices. The Church of England has appointed them as official diocesan record offices, and churches of other denominations also deposit their records there. Indeed, the availability of church records is greater now, as record offices have put more effort into collecting them, and the major churches have been encouraging local congregations to deposit their records.

Naturally enough, the quantity of church records is greater after about 1850, but there are a number of churches whose records do extend back considerably earlier.

Churchwardens' accounts

These are a particular type of record from the parishes of the Church of England. The churchwardens were ecclesiastical officials responsible for the maintenance of much of the fabric of the parish church, churchyard and other parish property. There were usually two of them elected annually from the parishioners.

They were also responsible for other financial affairs of the parish, including payments for the relief of the poor in the seventeenth and eighteenth centuries, and payments for fuel and parish salaries in the nineteenth. They also collected pew rents, which until the late nineteenth century were a regular feature of church practice. Until the mid-nineteenth century, there were some secular duties as well, including representing the views of parishioners in parochial matters.

With such a range of responsibilities, the accounts kept by churchwardens were usually very thorough and are a valuable source for a number of purposes. Their value for tracing our rural ancestors lies in the wide range of people that can be named in them. These can include the tradesmen with whom the parish dealt – the masons, carpenters, glaziers and their labourers who undertook work on the buildings, and bakers and shopkeepers who supplied bread, wine and candles for church services. The poor to whom payments were made might enter the accounts by name, as also some of those from whom pew rents were collected. From these we can gain some insights into the people of the parish and their different status.

Churchwardens' accounts include lists of the ratepayers in the parish; a good set will include the amount they paid. They are held in many local record offices. Local record societies have transcribed and published a number of them, while more recently efforts have been made to publish the transcripts on the internet. Some are available through British History Online, and using a search engine will reveal others.

Copyhold records

Copyhold was a form of manorial tenure, the record of which was maintained on the court rolls (see below *Court records*). Gradually land held by copyhold was converted to leasehold or freehold, and in 1841 an Act of Parliament established a nationally-administered procedure for the conversion ('enfranchisement' it was called) of copyhold land to freehold. The records are in the National Archives and provide some information about the tenants.

Coroners' records

Survival of the record of coroners' inquisitions is incomplete, and they are mostly to be found in county record offices. Where they do survive they can provide information, not only about the deceased, but also names and status of the jurors, witnesses, and some background to village life. Some collections of coroners' papers have been published by family and local history societies.

Court records

Court records can provide a great deal of information about rural people and society. Before the many reforms to local government in the nineteenth century, the business of the courts ranged widely, dealing with administrative matters as well as criminal.

The manorial courts of medieval and early modern times dealt with a wide range of administrative concerns of the manor as well lesser criminal offences (see also *Manorial records* below). There were two courts, the court baron and the court leet, each creating its set of records, the court rolls. Both were presided over by the lord of the manor or his steward. Other members of the two courts were often the same, and in their final years meetings of the court leet and the court baron were sometimes not easily distinguishable from one another.

The court baron enforced the customs of the manor and was a private perquisite of the lord. It dealt with matters to do with land and inheritance – these were the courts in which copyhold tenancies were registered. Many financial transactions, such as debt payments, came before the courts: disputes between neighbours; the regulation of farming in the common fields. The court appointed the reeve and beadle or bailiff, who looked after the lord's interests in the manor, the hayward, and some other posts, such as the swineherd and woodward. There were personal matters brought to the court, such as marriages, births out of wedlock among bondwomen, the departure from the village by a villein without prior permission.

The court leet dealt with public affairs of the manor: petty crime, and what would now be called anti-social behaviour, the infringement of bye-laws, and business licensing matters such as the assize of ale and bread.

Zvi Razi is a historian who has studied the court records and concluded that it is 'hard to conceive how a villager could have avoided appearing before the court from time to time' (*Life Marriage and Death in a Medieval Parish*, p. 2). The richer villagers – those who might have more property to contest – were more frequently in attendance than the poor. Women and minors were less often mentioned. But a remarkable amount of information about village society can be gained from these records, making them invaluable for tracing rural ancestors before about 1700. From the eighteenth century onwards the business of the manorial courts declined. Most of the work was transferred to other public courts; enclosure took away the role of managing the commons and open fields. The administration of copyhold land tenancy was the principal role left, and that work was also declining as leasehold tenure became more common.

Reading the manor court rolls, however, is not always a light matter. Medieval records were written on parchment scrolls and usually in Latin, with numerous shorthand abbreviations; from the sixteenth century they were generally compiled in book form and increasingly written in English. The parish registers, introduced in 1538, often provide an easier entry to the basic outline of village families for the early modern period, but for further information it can be worth persevering with the court rolls.

Manorial court records are quite plentiful. Most are held in The National Archives, and a number of others have been deposited in local record offices. The Manorial Documents Register is a record of known extant manorial documents. It was set up under the Law of Property Act 1922, which abolished copyhold tenure, and is maintained by the

National Register of Archives. The records included in the register under the terms of the Act are: 'court rolls, surveys, maps, terriers, documents and books of every description relating to the boundaries, wastes, customs or courts of a manor'. The register may be accessed through the National Archives, and is the means of finding whether the records for a particular locality survive.

Some manorial court rolls have been published. For sample extracts, these are two of several books:

Mark Bailey (ed.), *The English manor, c.1200–c.1500* (2002)
Ralph Evans, *Manorial economy and society in the later middle ages: selected documents in English translation* (1998)

Other court records of value are those of Quarter Sessions (see below), which also cover a mixture of judicial and administrative business. For serious offences, records of trial at the assizes will be useful, the records for which are held in the National Archives. The National Archives also hold records relating to the transportation of convicts to the colonies. This sentence was in force from 1787 to 1868 and often handed down to country people for offences ranging from poaching to involvement in the Swing riots of 1830.

Criminal records

The National Archives holds registers of criminals in England and Wales. A database of registers from 1791 to 1892 is available through the website of Ancestry.co.uk.

Diaries and reminiscences

Diaries and reminiscences are sources mainly for the nineteenth and twentieth centuries, although there are some from the eighteenth century, mainly written by members of what we might call the 'literary' classes – the country parson, for example. Rev Henry White, the brother of Gilbert White who wrote about the natural history of Selborne, was the incumbent at Fyfield, Hampshire, and his diary for 1780 survives.

In total, diaries are not particularly numerous: most people do not keep a diary, and of those that are written, most are lost.

Archives of farms may include some documents described as farm diaries. That is what they are: by the later nineteenth century they were often written in standard printed diaries bought from stationers. Most of them, however, are more in the nature of journals of the work on the farm. This is a typical entry from such a diary. It is for 6 May 1909 and from a farm in Berkshire:

Cultivating land by cowhouse
Rolled mangels in Lower field
Hoeing peas. Finished harrowing wheat
Turned the cows out to grass

The substance varies. Some move beyond the sparse information about farm work to add notes on the weather, some about the work individual labourers were doing, and people the farmer met at market. Some refer to the farmer's 'extra-curricular' activities, such as attendance at the Board of Guardians. There is one written by a farmer at Chieveley, Berkshire, who was on the committee organizing the village celebrations for Queen Victoria's jubilee in 1887. His diary entries tell us who attended the meetings, but nothing about their content. But this type of information is very valuable for the family historian – more so than the diary of farm operations. Even if your ancestor is not mentioned, it is possible to gain a bit of additional information about the daily round in the countryside, and some of the business and social interactions of the farmer who wrote the diary.

Even more can be gained from what one might think of as 'proper' diaries – those with a reasonably full entry about what the farmer was doing, even what he thought. They are much less common, but some of those that do exist have been published, and they are certainly worth tracking down to gain an insight into farming life of the nineteenth century and later. The nineteenth-century diaries of Cornelius Stovin provide much information about the social connections among the class of large farmers of the Lincolnshire Wolds where he lived. This diary has been published, and it is listed in the bibliography together with one or two other examples.

Diaries written by village tradesmen are of similar rarity. The diaries of Robert Stone, who was a miller at Pangbourne, Berkshire, in the 1870s survive in the collections of the Museum of English Rural Life. They give a very full account of his apprenticeship, his four-year courtship of his wife, his church life, as well as the work of milling.

Reminiscences are a different class of document. Diaries are written more or less at the time of the event, but reminiscences and memoirs are produced later, often considerably later, and are subject to the vagaries of memory. They fall into three broad categories.

First is the reminiscence written for publication. There is, needless to say, a great deal of this literature published in the twentieth century, a fair proportion of which extends the story back into the nineteenth.

Second, there are the recollections written not for publication. These tend to have less editorial intervention than the published variety. Most, but not all, are written mainly for the benefit of the author's family. It is worth asking around your family to find out if anyone has undertaken such a task. Many authors in more recent times have put a copy in their local record office or library just in case the original gets lost. It is very good that they do so, for these documents often have information of value beyond the immediate family.

This type of document can come from a wide social spectrum, at least from the late nineteenth century onwards. Charles Slater of Barley in Hertfordshire was an agricultural labourer born in 1868. 'I have now received the old age pension and I now look back on my 65 years', he wrote in his reminiscences of village life, which are preserved in their manuscript form. He begins in the 1870s and includes such developments as the arrival of the first motor cars in the village. He wrote in a more or less continuous stream, and the context of some of the things described is not always clear. This demonstration of the fallibility of memory is one of many things the historian needs to be aware of. Comparing the reminiscence with other sources is a useful precaution.

A third category is the oral history reminiscence, which might survive as a transcript or as a tape recording. This type of record needs to be read (or listened to) with as much care as the written family account. It is easy, for example, to lose sense of chronology, as interviewees often fail to mention dates or other fixed points of reference. One can get lost in a general flow of remembrances, which are not always well-connected. The interviewers also vary from the professional to the untrained, and this affects the quality of the replies. If you decide to undertake recordings of members of your family it is worth seeking advice on how to conduct the interview; a dry run without the recorder is one worthwhile ploy, to help hone the structure of the questions.

Many record offices and local studies libraries have collections of oral history, some dating back as far as the 1930s, but most from the 1960s onwards. Older examples tend to be one-off recordings, but more recently local groups have been running systematic projects involving larger numbers. Some professional recordings are included in the collections: the Museum of English Rural Life has some examples produced by Radio 210, a broadcaster in Berkshire and Hampshire, about village life and people.

There are now many published reminiscences. Farmers, farmers' wives, land girls and farmworkers, gamekeepers, journalists and politicians all have written about their lives in the country. Some have been written especially for publication, others published retrospectively.

Diocesan records

Diocesan records of the Church of England have much to tell us about the clergy and some of their parishioners. They include records of ordination and the work of the ecclesiastical courts. Another major class of record is the visitation returns, which are the reports following a formal episcopal visit to a parish. These can contain information about the incumbent and other officers, as well as comment on the state of the church, glebe land and the parish in general.

Records for many dioceses go back as far as the sixteenth century. Most are in the official diocesan record offices (county or other major record offices), although some have ended up in other places.

Directories

Trade directories were first published at the end of the eighteenth century. They provided some basic information about the principal towns of a county, including size, markets, main transport links, together with lists of leading inhabitants and trades. During succeeding decades directories grew larger to encompass the whole county, villages as well as towns. More general information about the counties was included, such as essays about their history and geology, along with detail about local government, postal services and so on.

Many different publishers entered this market. Some published directories for the larger towns, such as Reffold's Manchester Directory of the 1770s; others covered a wider area, usually a county. The leading publication initially was Pigot's, or the *Universal* directory. Pigot's publications had a more or less national coverage. He was joined by others, two of which also published directories for almost the whole country, while others remained local or regional in scope. William White's county directories of the mid-nineteenth century were among the more substantial. Frederick Kelly worked for the Post Office and started compiling directories to aid his work and as a publishing venture. Kelly became the publisher of the official *Post Office Directory*. These came to dominate the market, seeing off most of the competition by the 1870s. Kelly's directories ceased to have the Post Office appellation, but continued to dominate the market, especially for the county and rural districts. By the 1930s telephone directories were beginning to provide another means for finding people and businesses. County and trade directories continued to be published for some time, but Kelly's finally ceased publication in the 1960s.

Unlike the telephone directories which supplanted them, publication of Kelly's or the Post Office directories was not annual. There was no set pattern, publication being determined probably by the process of revision. Kelly's were published as county volumes, but often two or three counties would be bound together – Essex and Suffolk, for example. Larger towns and cities had their own directories. As well as the county and the town directories, there were a few comprehensive directories for certain trades published at the end of the nineteenth and beginning of the twentieth century. Most cover the more urban industries, such as engineering, but there are some with information for the seeker after rural forebears. The directory of the brewing, wine and spirits trades, for example, was published in 1902 when there were still many country brewers and maltsters to be found.

Directories are relatively ephemeral items, and their survival as a result is variable. However, record offices and local studies libraries hold copies of directories for their area, while specialist libraries and university libraries are likely to have a more wide-ranging coverage. The biggest collection is in the Guildhall Library in London, at Aldermanbury, London EC2V 7HH.

The Historical Directories Project
The Historical Directories Project at the University of Leicester is a digital collection of trade directories published in England and Wales between 1750 and 1919. It gives a comprehensive coverage of the country but it cannot include every one of the many thousands of directories published. Instead there are selected time periods – the 1850s, 1890s and 1910s – for which the project has produced a national map and at least one complete directory for each part of the country. For the rest of the time period sample directories have been digitized.

The project can be found at: http://www.historicaldirectories.org

Emigration

For rural ancestors who left the country, the best starting point is the National Archives, which has produced a research guide, available online and in printed form, to the sources it holds. Local studies can also be useful. For example, the Ryedale Folk Museum has copies of a study into the farmers and labourers who left the North York Moors for Canada.

Enclosure records

The enclosures of open fields, especially those carried out under Act of Parliament in the eighteenth and nineteenth centuries, have left a number of records which can help us find out about those involved. There is information about the leading promoters of enclosure, the people who surveyed the parish land, the occupiers of the land before and after the process. The documentation falls into a number of distinct categories: the parliamentary proceedings, including petitions against the Bill, and the final Act; the enclosure process described in surveys and reports, including those involved and how much it cost; the final enclosure award, together with a map.

Not all the records survive for every enclosure, but there is a good deal for most. They are to be found in a number of places. The House of Lords Record Office has many of the 'top copies' of the enclosure awards, and others are in the National Archives. Copies of awards and maps are in county record offices, although their collections are not always complete. However, these offices will be the most useful starting point for most searches.

Some digitization has been done on enclosure records to make information available online. One of the notable projects has been undertaken by the Berkshire Record Office. Called 'New Landscapes', it gives online access to most of the surviving enclosure awards and maps for the county, and a very good guide to enclosure records as a whole. The project can be found at www.berkshireenclosure.org.uk.

A guide to the maps is Roger J P Kain, John Chapman and Richard Oliver, *The Enclosure Maps of England and Wales, 1595–1918* (2004).

Estate agents' records

As mentioned in chapter 5, many landowners employed independent estate agency practices to manage their estates. Records from some of these practices can be found in county record offices, and they can provide information about the tenants of an estate, and others with whom it had dealings, sometimes filling in gaps where the estate owner's records have been lost.

Estate records

The landowners of England and Wales generated large quantities of records which are invaluable sources for the history of rural life. Because of the relative stability of landed society, the survival rate of these records is remarkably high.

The records can be grouped into two main types. There are records of estate management, often the largest part. These include accounts, rentals and surveys, records of building repairs, and correspondence conducted on behalf of the estate, usually by the steward or agent.

As sources for family history, this class of documents can provide information about people who worked for the estate – the agent who managed the whole, as well as bailiffs, gamekeepers and others. The records can also be informative about the tenants, making up in some respects for the lack of records from farmers. Estate rentals list the tenants, the farms they held and the rent they paid for them. A good series of rentals can give quite precise information about when a farmer came on to his farm, when he left, and changes in between. Estate surveys go into

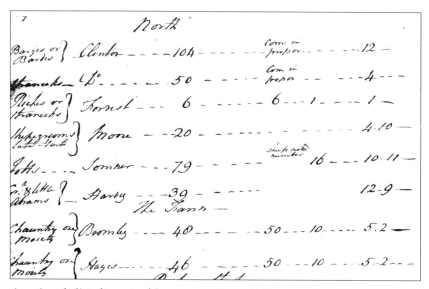

A section of a list of tenants of Orsett estate, Essex, 1800. (Museum of English Rural Life)

more detail about the farms and their composition. Tenancy agreements are documents that drew up terms and conditions under which the farmer held the land from the estate. Correspondence survives less frequently, but when it does it can be revealing about relations between farmers and the estate.

The second group of records created by the landed estates is the household accounts and associated records. These often reveal a lot about the lives of the landed family. Essex Record Office, for example, has a collection of bills and receipts – about 40,000 of them – from Audley End. Dated between 1765 and 1832, they are in neat bundles labelled 'glazier', 'carpenter', 'coal', 'saddler', and so on. There is information to be had there about some of the tradesmen with whom the estate and household dealt, although some patience is required to study them. Besides these, household accounts can provide information about some of the cooks, butlers, footmen and maids who worked in and around the house.

The records have not survived for every landed estate by any means, but a remarkable number have, ranging from the greatest ducal estates to the modest gentry acres. Some families have retained their estate and family papers, others are in the hands of the current owners of the land, and yet more have been deposited in county record offices, universities and other public repositories. Nearly all are available for study. The National Register of Archives is the place to find out whether records from an estate survive and their whereabouts. The Register is available through the National Archives.

Family papers

Most of us can say we have family papers now – personal and family correspondence, photograph albums, diaries and memorabilia. Not many of us have deposited them in record offices (to the relief, perhaps, of archivists!). But this serves to remind us that, although landowners are by far the greatest source of personal and family papers, the range does extend more widely across society.

Farm records

Farm records do not survive in great numbers. In the early 1960s the Museum of English Rural Life carried out a survey project to discover what farm records there were. This was at a time when none to speak of had reached record offices. The result of this project was that the museum gathered a collection of records from about a thousand farms. More have

Part of a farm account book for West Monkton Farm, Tarrant Monkton, Dorset. This page shows the labourers and the wages paid to them for a week in June 1858. (Museum of English Rural Life)

been added since, both to the collections at the museum and to the archives at other record offices, but these still represent a small fraction of the total number of farmers.

Although there are not many of them, farm accounts do extend well back in time. For example, Robert Loder's farm accounts from Berkshire and Henry Best's from Yorkshire are from the seventeenth century; both have been published. They give valuable insights into the workings of farm and household. For example, from Robert Loder's accounts, the originals of which are in Berkshire Record Office, we learn that his household contained eight people: Loder, his wife, two children, two male living-in servants, and two female.

Farmers' clubs and agricultural societies

In 1838 the English Agricultural Society was founded by a group of leading farmers and landowners with the Earl Spencer as its first president. A couple of years later the Queen granted it a royal charter; it became the Royal Agricultural Society of England, and still exists today, with headquarters at Stoneleigh in Warwickshire.

The Royal Agricultural Society, with its national membership, was the grandest of the agricultural societies, but there were many more, often considerably older. The Society of Arts (full name the Society for the Encouragement of Arts, Manufactures and Commerce) was founded in 1754 and had interests in agriculture, and the Smithfield Club, a society promoting improvement in stock-raising, was founded in 1798. There were many regional and local groups. The Bath & West of England Society, founded in 1777 with a wide regional remit, was the best known of these, but a good fifty societies had been established by 1820. Each held their shows, ploughing matches and other events.

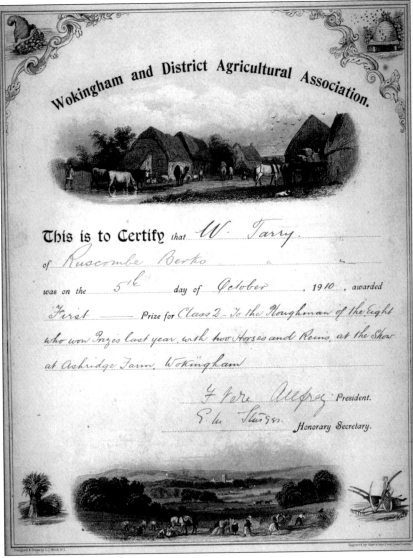

A ploughing match certificate awarded to William Tarry of Ruscombe, Berkshire in 1910. (Museum of English Rural Life)

Archives survive from several of these societies. Both the Royal and the Bath & West have good records of membership and committees. The Royal's are in part at the Museum of English Rural Life, with more recent documents still with the society. The Bath & West retain their archives. Winners of prizes were published in their journals. Survival of records from local societies is variable, but show certificates and medals often turn up in museums even if other documents have been lost. A few societies have had their history written up. There is a bicentenary volume for the Bath & West, and one for the 150th anniversary of the Royal Agricultural Society, while Lincolnshire county and Wokingham (Berkshire) district societies have both had books written about them.

Farmers' unions

The National Farmers' Union might not regard itself as a trade union nevertheless its records are similar. The union was founded in 1908, building on the foundations of a union for the county of Lincolnshire established a few years earlier. Records of its main executive and committees survive for the first forty years or so of the union's existence. These are held by the Museum of English Rural Life. Detailed membership records do not survive, but some of the minute books can be useful sources of information about those who were involved in committee work, and the house journals can yield information about members. From the 1950s onwards, the survival rate of the union's archives is less good. A book on the first hundred years of the union was published in 2008: Guy Smith, *From Campbell to Kendall.*

The records of local branches of the union do sometimes contain subscription and membership books, as well as minutes, newsletters and other documents. Not every branch preserved its records, but those that have survived are mostly in local record offices, for example, the Cheshire and Chester Archives hold records of the county branch and a number of local branches in the county.

Friendly society records

Village friendly societies were numerous, and most of them were small. Many lasted until well into the twentieth century, giving a chance for some documentation to survive, and this might include membership records and minute books. While many village societies were wound up, others amalgamated with one of the larger societies, such as the Oddfellows, with whose records the village society's might be found. The records of others have been deposited in county and local record offices. Local newspapers often reported the activities of the friendly societies. Other documents, such as photographs, might be found in museum collections. One of the traditions of the friendly societies was an annual parade, service and meal, and many memorabilia can be found, such as the decorated brass heads from the poles carried in the parades. The Museum of English Rural Life has a fine collection of these pole heads from Somerset societies.

Regulation of friendly societies was administered locally by the quarter sessions until nineteenth-century legislation set up the Registrar of Friendly Societies. The records of the Registrar are held in The National Archives.

If you are interested in further study of the societies there is a Friendly Societies Research Group at the Open University, which encourages research and the preservation of records. Their website www.open.ac.uk/socialsciences/friendly-societies-research-group/ is a useful introduction to the subject.

Good books to start a study of the societies include Roger Logan, *An Introduction to Friendly Society Records* (2000), while Simon Cordery, *British Friendly Societies 1750–1914* (2003), provides an introduction to the societies themselves.

Gamekeepers' registers

Registers of gamekeepers were maintained from 1711 to 1889, a legal requirement. They record the name of the keeper and the lord of the manor who 'deputed' the power of killing game.

Hearth tax

A tax levied on every hearth in all property was introduced in England in 1662 and continued until 1689. It is regarded by some as one of the best sources of population and genealogical information before the introduction of the census. By no means all the records survive, but there is at least one full list for each county in England and Wales. The tax returns list the property owners, not all the inhabitants. The hearth tax records are in The National Archives.

A guide to the collection and a basic database are available through their website. A guide in book form is: J Gibson, *The Hearth Tax and other later Stuart Tax Lists* (1996), and volumes in the *Victoria County History* also contain useful introductory guidance. Much work has gone into transcribing and indexing hearth tax returns, and many have been published, including some online. Using a search engine will be a good way of finding them.

Inquisitions post mortem

These records were created on the death of a feudal tenant in chief, that is, a direct tenant of the crown. They were an inquiry into what lands the tenant held and who was entitled to succeed him. Although they related directly to the tenant in chief, the inquisitions do contain some incidental references to others who might be of interest to family historians. They can also help in tracing descent of property in the medieval and early modern periods. The records exist from 1240 to 1660, when feudal tenure was abolished. Most of these records are held in The National Archives.

Land tax

A tax on the value of land was introduced as an emergency measure in 1692 to raise revenue for the war with France. It remained as a permanent fixture until 1798, although it had to be voted annually by Parliament. In 1798 it was made a permanent tax, not subject to annual vote, but landowners could redeem it on payment of a lump sum. Gradually the tax was redeemed, although the remaining unredeemed tax was not abolished until 1963.

Many land tax assessments survive, held in county and local record offices. The assessments give the names of the owner or occupier of the land subject to tax and a description of the land. There are many difficulties in interpreting the records, but these affect mainly their analysis for such purposes as land values and agricultural production. They are also variable in their completeness, and as a measure of the wealth of the taxpayer, because landowners could find many ways to avoid the tax or at least get their assessment reduced. They are especially inaccurate for small holdings of land.

For the family historian the main purpose of land tax records is to trace the names of those who held land, and what the holding was. They can be used in conjunction with estate records or other property records, but where those are lacking, the land tax assessment becomes a valuable source on its own. It is worth bearing in mind the inaccuracies, but most problems need not trouble the family researcher, unless you are drawn to investigate further some aspect of your ancestor's life.

Manorial records

'Manor', from the Latin for house, was a term introduced by the Normans, and features in Domesday Book to denote an area under a local lord who held his land directly under the crown – an estate, or part of one, because one lord might hold several manors. The size and extent of the manor varied considerably. Sometimes the manor was equivalent to the village, but some manors encompassed two or more villages, while other smaller manors covered part of a village only. The lord was granted jurisdiction over all the tenants of his manor – the feudal tenants owing customary services and the free tenants paying rent. This meant that manorial records had a double function. They were the record of estate and of local administration, the distinction between the two, of course, not being recognized by contemporaries. The manor was administered by the reeve, assisted by the hayward, beadle and other men. They reported to the bailiff who looked after two or three manors, and he in turn was under the estate steward.

The breaking down of feudal tenure, formally abolished in 1660, separated title to land from the lordship of the manor. Lordships became objects of commerce, bought and sold along with other property. The landowning classes usually owned the lordships of manors: thus it is common to find in nineteenth-century directories the statement that 'the principal landowner and lord of the manor' of the parish were the same. That was not universal, however: of Skendleby in Lincolnshire in the mid-nineteenth century, 'Lord Willoughby de Eresby is patron, impropriator and lord of the manor, but a great part of the soil belongs to Sir Edward Brakenbury, John Holland, Esq., and a few smaller proprietors.'

The continued existence of manorial tenure, especially in the form of copyhold, meant that the manor still had a role as an administrative unit. Changes to estate administration during the eighteenth century, the conversion of copyhold tenure to leasehold and freehold, and the transfer of its jurisdictional responsibilities to others, such as the overseers, churchwardens and quarter sessions, effectively rendered the manor redundant as an administrative body. Yet manorial courts continued to meet for some time, if only as a matter of form, several existing well into the nineteenth century. The abolition of all remaining manorial tenures in 1925 to establish the forms of freehold and leasehold with which we are now familiar, finally completed the divorce between title to lordship and function. Even so, a handful of manor courts still meet once a year –

there are three or four in the North York Moors. As a source of records, for the times before the manor's decline manorial documents are the richest as far as a source of information for genealogical study is concerned. Do not be put off by some of the terminology used – leet,

Manor of Orsett			
Name of Tenant	Date of Admission	Property	Present Tenant
Wm Sackett	21st July 1817	Slade Hold	This Mr W Sackett has been dead some years so there is no Tenant on the Rolls It should be the Churchwardens Capt. Whitmore W H Sackett
Mary Dawson	21st July 1817	Wheat field & Clover field called Tap Steps 2 Index	Present tenant G. E. Dawson Esq Jos 10 Hart Street Bloomsbury not admitted
James Hutchings	28th July 1829	Jolly Cocks party hurdles hm	Rev. Jas Hutchings % Savill & Son Messr Savill & Son act as his Agent
George Mawson	4th Decr 1829	Gillmans	Rev. Jas Hutchings Messr Savill & Son act as his Agent

List of tenants of the Manor of Orsett, c1890. (Museum of English Rural Life)

The court leet of the Manor of Spaunton in North Yorkshire still meets, and has adapted to modern concerns. (The author)

custumal, view of frankpledge, quit rental – deriving from the medieval lawyer's jargon.

The double function of the manor's administration means that the records are both valuable and have survived quite well. The central institution of the manor was the court, from which court rolls (see above *Court records*) often survive. Among the other records generated by the manor were the descriptions and valuations of the land, its tenants and rents, variously called surveys, custumals and extents.

Manorial records are to be found in many archives. The National Archives holds the major collections of manorial records, while county record offices have additional collections. The modern landed estate incorporated many manorial lands, and copies of manorial documents, such as surveys and rentals are often found in estate papers.

Maps and plans

Maps are invaluable: they can set the context of our family history research, and often show precisely where our ancestors lived and worked. The Ordnance Survey began publishing its maps at one inch to the mile in 1801 – Kent was the first sheet issued. Other notable series were the six-inch maps of the 1880s and 25-inch maps introduced in the 1890s.

The commutation of tithes resulted in a major survey and mapping exercise carried out in the late 1830s and 1840s. Other maps and plans were produced during the nineteenth century in connection with the construction of railways, water works and other public utilities, many of which affected life in the countryside.

Enclosure maps and estate maps and plans offer documents for the eighteenth century, sometimes earlier. More than 20,000 estate maps dating from before 1850 are known, a remarkably large number.

The British Library's map collections are very large, with full national sets of Ordnance Survey maps. However, record offices and local studies

A map of the Manor of Winsley in Wiltshire in the eighteenth century. On this scale of reproduction only a general impression of the nature of these documents can be conveyed. (Museum of English Rural Life)

libraries are often the best starting points for collections of maps for the area we are studying. Some maps, including some of the nineteenth-century series of Ordnance Survey maps, are available digitally and online (the Old Maps website, www.old-maps.co.uk, is one place to look) though it has to be said that this is one area where the screen does not always adequately substitute for the real thing.

Memorials and monuments

A common pastime for many a researcher of family history is to wander round graveyards studying the inscriptions on burial stones. There are often plot records for the larger municipal cemeteries of the towns, but less frequently so for the village churchyard. Local and family history societies have in a number of instances taken on the painstaking work of recording parish grave inscriptions. They have usually published the results, and some are now being made available online. It is worth checking the societies local to the area of your study.

The interior of churches often have memorial inscriptions, and to a surprisingly wide range of people, not only the local landowner. Not all churches are open to the casual visitor, especially the non-Anglican ones, and it is worth enquiring before making a long journey especially to view the church.

Another monument in the village is the war memorial, erected in the 1920s to record the names of villagers who fell in the First World War, to which have often been added those from the Second World War, and sometimes later conflicts.

Newspapers and magazines

Local newspapers can be a mine of information about village life. They give reports about farming, including local markets, the progress of the harvest, and hiring fairs. Although much of this type of information is of an impersonal nature – the reports of the hiring fair, for example – there are many occasions when individual names are mentioned. They often tend to be exceptional incidents – labourer gets his arm caught in the threshing machine, and the like – and the people involved in misdemeanours. Local papers in the twentieth century begin to take up the 'personal interest' stories, reporting individuals involved in charity events, for example. The advertising can also be a useful source, providing information on businesses in the countryside and on properties for sale or to let, for example.

The war memorial in Rosedale Abbey churchyard, North Yorkshire. Erected after the First World War, it has had the names of those of the village who were killed in the Second World War and Korean War added subsequently. (The author)

Newspapers originated during the seventeenth century, but it was in the late eighteenth and nineteenth centuries that local newspapers came into their own. They increased in number and in size, especially after taxation was removed from newspapers in 1855 (it had been reduced from 4d to 1d in 1836), and in the strength of their local coverage. They continued to reprint national news (most of their readers did not take a national paper before the end of the nineteenth century) but, with more pages, could give better local information.

Publishers of newspapers were based in the towns, but covered the area around them, some with a more restricted area than others. Epworth, in the Isle of Axholme, had its local paper, the *Epworth Bells*, which rarely strayed beyond the Isle in its interests. In contrast, the *Lincoln, Rutland and Stamford Mercury*, one of the oldest local papers, founded in 1713, was of a more regional nature, reporting on the whole of Lincolnshire and Rutland, and a good part of Northamptonshire, Nottinghamshire and Huntingdonshire as well.

The British Library holds the largest collection of newspapers from around the kingdom. Many have been digitized, but not all are available free through the internet. Information about the digital resources is on the library's website at http://newspapers.bl.uk/blcs/. The newspaper library itself is in Colindale, north London, a few steps from the Underground station. Its postal address is British Library Newspapers, Colindale Avenue, London NW9 5HE. Telephone 0207 412 7353.

For local sources, the main libraries, such as the local studies library, are able to help locate runs of newspapers. Some are still available in original form, but often they are microfilm, or sometimes digital copies. A consortium of libraries and record offices in the East Midlands has developed the Newsplan project, which has produced a useful database of newspapers published in this region and their holdings in local and national libraries. It can be found at http://newsplan.liem.org.uk.

Specialist journals for the world of farming and the countryside can be traced back to the *Gentleman's Magazine*, first published in 1731, and the *Annals of Agriculture*, published from 1784 to 1815. More were founded during the nineteenth century. They included journals such as *The Farmer's Magazine* published in the mid-nineteenth century, and weeklies, such as *Mark Lane Express*, which also catered for a farming readership. They have been succeeded by such twentieth-century titles as *Farmer & Stockbreeder* and *Farmers' Weekly*.

One of the lesser-known country journals, The Country Standard *championed the small farmer and the agricultural worker.* (Museum of English Rural Life)

Some of the early journals are available online. Ancestry.co.uk has a searchable database for the *Gentleman's Magazine,* while early volumes can be viewed through the Bodleian Library's website at www.bodley.ox. ac.uk/ilej. The *Annals of Agriculture* is available through http://www. archive.org/details/annalsofagricult01londuoft.

Obituaries

One of the features in newspapers and magazines that can be very useful for family research is the obituary – or, occasionally, a tribute to someone still living. Coverage can be very uneven: I once spent some time searching for a farmer who was quite notable in his time, for whom I was quite sure there would be an obituary, but I was disappointed. On the other hand we can find unexpected tributes. Obituaries need to be handled with care, as their writers did not always have the full facts, and errors occasionally creep in.

Official sources

Agriculture and rural life have been the subject of a number of government and parliamentary enquiries. Select committees of the houses of parliament and royal commissions are the most common of these. Their proceedings usually include sessions in which people are called to give evidence. Those giving the evidence are named, while other people may be recorded by name from time to time. The minutes, records of other proceedings and reports are printed in official publications. These, together with the printed Bills and Acts of Parliament and other publications, are known collectively as Parliamentary Papers.

Among the papers that can be useful for study of rural ancestors are the reports of the Poor Law Commission in 1834, the Royal Commission on the Employment of Women and Children in Agriculture, which reported in 1867, and the Royal Commission on Agricultural Depression, which sat between 1893 and 1897.

There are a number of printed indexes to the Parliamentary Papers, which can be seen in large research libraries such as the universities. Chadwyck-Healey, one of the publishers of these, has an online index to the House of Commons Papers. It can be seen at: http://parlipapers. chadwyck.co.uk/marketing/index.jsp. It is a subscription service, but record offices and libraries are often subscribers, and it is possible to look at the index there.

The British Library has a useful guide to the Parliamentary Papers at this rather long address:

http://www.bl.uk/reshelp/findhelprestype/offpubs/ukofficalpub/parl papers/parliamentpapers.pdf

There have been a number of projects initiated at universities in recent years to digitize some of the Parliamentary Papers. The best way to find out about progress and the availability of the results will be through search engines.

Photographs

The photograph was an invention of the 1830s. For the first few decades it was the preserve of the professional or the wealthy amateur who could afford the large cameras and other equipment. The introduction of cheap compact cameras from the 1880s, followed by roll film, opened up photography to everybody. All could now have their family album of snapshots, as the numbers of photographs, taken by amateurs and professionals alike, increased enormously.

The family collection of photographs is an invaluable source for likenesses of our ancestors, and often the context in which they worked and spent their leisure. They are, however, vulnerable documents, always

The owner of the Sulham estate in Berkshire was a keen amateur photographer. He took this one of two women outside their dwellings in the 1890s. (Museum of English Rural Life)

in danger from the household clear-out after the funeral. Photographs are now a common part of the collections in record offices and museums. Some are to be found in personal and family papers, others in the records of professional photographers. Some professionals made a speciality of the countryside, rural people and events, submitting their work to press agencies, publishers and magazines. Finding our ancestors depicted in the collections of photographs in record offices and museums is always going to be open to chance. On the other hand, the photographs provide much useful information about rural life in the nineteenth and twentieth centuries.

Poll tax

This is the poll tax of the fourteenth century, levied in 1377, 1379 and 1381. The records of this tax are valuable sources for genealogy in the medieval period. Although the poor were exempt, which does leave a large proportion of society unrepresented, returns generally give the names and residence of all who paid. Quite often family relationships are also noted. The records are in the National Archives and have been published in three volumes.

Probate inventories

In the second quarter of the sixteenth century the ecclesiastical courts began asking for a detailed inventory of the testator's possessions when the will was proved. This began in 1530, although it took a little while to become established practice, and continued until 1782. The document produced, known as the probate inventory, can be a valuable source of information. It has been used by economic and social historians to study the output of arable farming, developments in livestock farming and food in the seventeenth century. The inventory is no less valuable for the family historian in revealing much of the material background to an ancestor's life.

Probate inventories recorded the personal wealth of the testator, or at least the principal items: there is no guarantee that the list is complete. Certainly omitted were valuations of buildings and land. Debts owed and due were included.

Most often the inventory is to be found together with the will (see entry below on wills), although time has separated some from their will. Together, wills and inventories give information on people from a wide range of rural trades and backgrounds. There are not many from labourers, but some of those from tradesmen and farmers do give information about their employees.

There is a bibliography of probate inventories, published in 1983: Mark Overton, *A Bibliography of British Probate Inventories*. The National Archives hold large collections of probate inventories along with the wills, but copies can be found in many other record offices. Some sets of probate inventories have been published, and transcriptions of individual inventories can be found in local history journals.

Quarter Sessions records

Quarter Sessions were the meetings of the county justices of the peace held four times a year (as the name implies). The sessions were established in the fourteenth century and embraced both judicial and administrative functions. They lost their administrative role in 1889 on the formation of county councils, but their judicial function continued until 1972.

A few records date from the fourteenth and fifteenth centuries, but most surviving documents are from the seventeenth century and after. Judicial matters covered by the quarter sessions records included infringements of the poor laws, coroners' reports, licensing laws, all manner of felonies including theft, robbery and murder, and breaking the game laws. Administrative matters include jury and electoral registers, licences for alehouses and gamekeepers, supervision of the poor laws (including appointments of parish overseers), enclosure and land tax.

Most quarter sessions records are held in county record offices. A guide to them is Jeremy Gibson, *Quarter Sessions Records for Family Historians*.

Rates books

Until recently rates were the main form of local taxation, and they survive in a levy on businesses. The term, however, covers a wide range of locally-raised taxes from early modern times onwards. What they had in common was being based on property and the generation of 'rate books' to record those liable to pay the duty. The principal types of rates were the poor, church and highway rates. They were separate levies, and raised in the parishes. After the reform of the poor law in 1834 the Unions took over the poor assessment, and subsequent reforms of local government introduced the general rate in place of the specific ones.

Parish rate books were maintained by the churchwardens (see *Churchwardens' accounts* above), and the later books were in the hands of the local authorities. Almost all those that survive are in local record offices. The papers of individuals – farmers and tradesmen – quite often include some rate demands or receipts for payments.

Terriers

Terriers are surveys of the land, the name coming from the Latin *terrarius*. There are two types of archival document to which the term is attached – glebe terrier and manorial terrier.

Glebe terriers are surveys of the rectory or vicarage along with the associated glebe land. They were carried out in connection with episcopal visitations from about 1600 onwards. The tenants of the glebe lands will be entered, and sometimes additional information about tithes.

The manorial terrier (or extent) was a survey of the land of the manor, in more or less detail, but giving at least the name of the holders of manorial land and the extent of their holdings, if not their location. Most date from between 1550 and 1700. They are usually found in collections of estate papers. Some are called surveys, a name meaning more to the modern reader: the variations in name were the choice of the manorial officials.

Tithe records

Records relating to tithe disputes can be found in archives of diocesan courts, and in archives of the Chancery and Exchequer in The National Archives.

The commutation of tithe into a monetary payment in 1836 resulted in a major work of surveying 11,800 parishes in England and Wales undertaken by specially appointed commissioners. Three main series of records are available: the tithe map, on which every dwelling and field that was liable to tithe was plotted; the apportionment, listing the owners and occupiers of property and their new monetary liability; and general files of material gathered by tithe commissioners. National coverage is not complete, for not everywhere was subject to payment of tithe in kind by 1836.

The full series of documents are in The National Archives. Two copies of the maps and apportionments were made, one for the diocese and one for the incumbent of the parish. Many of these survive in the collections of local record offices, most often those that are appointed as diocesan record offices. Locally held records are not always complete, however.

Publications on the tithe and its records include:

Roger J P Kain and Hugh C Prince, *Tithe Surveys* (2000)
Roger J P Kain and Richard R Oliver, *The Tithe Maps of England and Wales*
  – a cartographic analysis and county-by-county catalogue (1995).

Title deeds

A title deed is a legal document setting out someone's right (title) to the land he owns. Deeds are therefore useful records for tracing the property our ancestors possessed. The Land Registry was established in 1862, and its records are being made available online. However, until very recently registration was not compulsory, and efforts are only now being made to get all the land in the country registered. It will be some time, therefore, before it will be possible to make a search by computer for every property. In the meantime, deeds retain their value in showing title to property, and the people involved in a land transfer.

Finding title deeds is no simple matter. They can be found in almost every record office, from The National Archives to local offices. They have been deposited by landowners, solicitors, mortgagees and others, and a deed may be in an office some distance from the property to which it relates. Many deeds are in private hands. There are a few registers of deeds: for Middlesex (in London Metropolitan Archives), for the three ridings of Yorkshire (in the record offices at Beverley, Northallerton and Wakefield) and for the Bedford Level of the Fens (in Cambridgeshire Record Office). Otherwise there are no general indexes for rural deeds. Beginning a search for deeds, therefore, is best done through Access to Archives through the National Archives' website.

Trade union records

The records of the National Union of Agricultural and Allied Workers are held at the Museum of English Rural Life. They consist mainly of accounts and minute books of the union's many committees. Records that relate to membership of the union and its branches are extremely limited before the 1970s.

The Transport and General Workers Union also had interests in farm workers, and a body of records from the 1920s to the 1990s is held by the Modern Records Centre at the University of Warwick. These again are mainly administrative and research papers. (http://modernrecords.warwick.ac.uk).

For tracing records of individuals, therefore, these archives are of limited value, but for wider background information on unions and their

Thomas Parker, a founder of the Warwickshire Agricultural Labourers' Union in 1872. (Museum of English Rural Life)

activities in support of their members, there is much more to be found. To take one example, there are files relating to the question of tied cottages, for long a contentious issue for rural workers.

Vestry records

The vestry was the decision-making body of the parish, its name deriving from the place in which it met. Some vestries were open to all, others were closed meetings mainly of the parish officials. The vestry took the important desicions about the parish and its finances, especially including the administration of the poor laws. The meeting of the vestry held at Easter set the parish poor rate, while discussions about how to deal with individual paupers are entered in the minutes. It is for the poor records that the vestry minutes and accounts are most valuable to family historians. They are to be found in county record offices.

Wills

Not everyone makes a will, of course, and in previous centuries the proportion of the population that did so was smaller – the lower down the social scale, the less likely one was to make a will. Farm labourers are thus unusual if they left a will, but farmers and village tradesmen, even of quite modest businesses often did. Where a will survives it can provide a wealth of information about the testator, his property and relationships with others. Servants, for example, were not infrequently beneficiaries, if only in a small way.

Since 1858 probate has been a civil matter administered through the courts – it is now the Family Division of the High Court. Copies of wills can be seen at the Court's reading room: Probate Department of the Principal Registry Family Division, Probate Search Room, First Avenue House, 42–49 High Holborn, London WC1V 6NP; telephone 0207 947 7000. Postal application for copies of wills, for which a fee is charged, can be made to The Postal Searches and Copies Department, York Probate Sub-Registry, Castle Chambers, Clifford Street, York YO1 9RG. Further details can be found on the website of HM Courts Service: www.hmcourts-service.gov.uk/infoabout/civil/probate/index.htm.

Indexes to post-1858 wills can be found through the Courts Service website, through local registry offices and local record offices. The National Archives also has a number of useful links to sources for wills.

Before 1858, wills were proved through church courts, which would when satisfied pass a Probate Act, endorse the will and give a copy to the executors. At the head of the hierarchy of ecclesiastical courts were the two provincial courts: the Prerogative Court of Canterbury and the Prerogative Court of York, to which records were eventually passed. Broadly speaking, those who lived in the northern province (as far south as Nottinghamshire) had their wills proved through York, those in the south and in Wales through Canterbury. However, since Canterbury had precedence over York, there are many instances of northern probate going to the southern court, especially if the deceased had property in both provinces. Canterbury wills (the records go back as far as 1384) are at the National Archives. They have been indexed and copied to view online at (www.nationalarchives.gov.uk/documentsonline/wills.asp? WT.hp=Wills). York wills are held at the Borthwick Institute; they are not all indexed, but the indexes so far completed are available through www.britishorigins.com, which is a subscription service.

As well as these major national sources, wills often can be found in family papers, and in the records of solicitors held in local archives.

In the seventeenth and eighteenth centuries, many wills also had probate inventories (see above).

Chapter 10

WHERE TO FIND INFORMATION

Getting started

If you are completely new to family history research there are a number of good introductory books to give you guidance. Among them are: Mark Pearsall, *Family history companion: fast-forward your family history search* (2007) and Dan Waddell, *Who do you think you are: the essential guide to tracing your family history* (2004). Two recent introductory books are *Starting out in Family History* (Pen and Sword 2010) and Nick Barratt, *Nick Barratt's Guide to Your Ancestors' Lives* (Pen and Sword 2010).

These will provide guidance in using the census returns, the parish registers and other sources, so that you can start to create your family tree. This process will soon reveal people who were your rural ancestors, about whom you might want to find out a bit more background information.

At the early stages of research you will want to talk to members of your family, seek out old photographs, and visit villages associated with your forebears. A preliminary visit to the local studies library to get the feel of some of the sources, such as directories, will be helpful.

None of these steps has needed a computer or the internet, and you might want to keep it that way. It is perfectly reasonable to conduct your family history research without possessing a computer. It has to be said, however, that you will probably need help from others who do. The last time the directory of record offices in the United Kingdom was issued in printed form, The National Archives was still called the Public Record Office. To find addresses and telephone numbers for the offices you might want to visit nowadays really needs the internet.

If you do have access to the internet, a very good starting point is the website of The National Archives (www.nationalarchives.gov.uk). There are some introductory research guides, in particular one entitled 'Family History in England and Wales'. This gives a basic introduction to the documents recording the population, such as the civil and parish registers of births, marriages and deaths. These are some of the basic tools for discovering who our family forebears were.

Record Offices

Many documents are held in county or local record offices, and the archives of universities and museums. Access to them is straightforward, but you usually have to show identification the first time you go. Many, especially the county record offices, have joined the 'CARN' scheme, which means that once you have signed on at one office you are issued with a card which provides the identification for the other member offices.

The National Archives

The National Archives at Kew, near London, is the repository for all public records created by central government. It houses the basic population records from the census.

The National Archives plays host to a number of national databases. First is the Archon directory of record offices (see below). Second is the National Register of Archives (www.nationalarchives.gov.uk/nra), which is a directory of major archival holdings throughout the nation. Third is Access to Archives (www.nationalarchives.gov.uk/a2a), which is an online national database of detailed archive catalogues. It is no longer accepting new catalogue records, however, so for the most up-to-date cataloguing it is necessary to go to the individual record offices.

Local Record offices

Record offices for the counties of England and Wales were established mainly in the first decade after the Second World War. Since then more local record offices have been established, often reflecting changes in local government, resulting in many cities and towns having their own local repositories.

The county record offices will be the principal ones for the study of our rural ancestors, but almost all offices are likely to hold some documents of interest, except the most metropolitan – and even they might contain some surprises among their collections. Documents relating to rural administration, such as the quarter sessions, poor law records and court rolls, are the main series to be found in the county archives. In addition there are estate, farm and business records from the local area.

County record offices and some of the major city archives (Manchester is an example) are also designated as diocesan record offices by the

Church of England. Parishes are now expected to deposit their archives with the appropriate diocesan record office.

The remit of these record offices is for their own local area, but archives do not always fit in so neatly. The great landowner might have land across several counties, the company might have a widespread business; we therefore have to be prepared to find that records are held in a record office out of area.

Contact details can most easily be found now through the internet. The Archon directory, hosted by the National Archives, gives links to all the archive repositories throughout the United Kingdom, where opening hours, addresses, telephone and email contacts can be found. Many offices now have catalogues available online. The Archon directory can be found at www.nationalarchives.gov.uk/archon.

Most county record offices subscribe to the CARN scheme, through which registration at any member office entitles the researcher to a card that is accepted at all other member offices. Whether or not the record office uses the CARN scheme, almost all will expect to see some form of identification on your first visit. It is always the best plan to book ahead for your visit to the archives. Sometimes they might be full, and non-booked people will be turned away, but giving the archivists notice means that they can prepare and have documents ready for you as soon as you arrive.

Specialist Record offices
There are some record offices that are specialists in the subject rather than for a particular district – 'special repositories' they are called in the jargon of the archives trade. Rural life and the countryside has its specialist record offices. The most important for England is the Museum of English Rural Life. It holds the largest collection of farm records in the country, the records of organizations such as the National Union of Agricultural and Allied Workers, and it also has one of the biggest libraries of countryside matters. Its address is Museum of English Rural Life, Redlands Road, Reading RG1 5EX, and on the internet it can be found at www.reading.ac.uk/merl. There is an online catalogue, although it does not yet include absolutely everything in the collections, so it is always worth asking if you do not see what you expected to find.

Libraries

The British Library

The British Library is the largest of the national libraries, holding a copy of nearly everything published in Britain, and much published overseas. It is invaluable for those books almost impossible to find elsewhere, especially books of the eighteenth century and earlier. It has copies of published transcripts of parish registers, directories, local history books and pamphlets. There is a large collection of maps and plans, and the newspaper collection covers the widest range of regional and local publications.

The British Library is at St Pancras, London. There is also a reading room at Boston Spa, Yorkshire. The newspaper library is in North London at Colindale (until 2012/13 when its collections are moved to St Pancras and Boston Spa). Some newspapers have been digitized, and these can be viewed on the computers in the other reading rooms.

The library's website at www.bl.uk includes a full online catalogue.

Local studies libraries

Local studies libraries are good places to start. They will have a range of introductory books on family history, local history, local biography, and so on. Directories, maps, newspapers, photographs and reference books on, for example, landowning families are among the other things to be found. Local studies librarians will also be able to guide you through the sources on the internet, if you do not have a computer or do not use the internet at home.

Specialist libraries

There are a number of libraries with special collections relating to agriculture and rural life. The Museum of English Rural Life has been mentioned above. In addition there are the libraries of the Royal Agricultural Society of England at Stoneleigh. The address is Royal Agricultural Society of England, Stoneleigh Park, Warwickshire, CV8 2LZ. Its website is www.rase.org.uk. Select the 'What we do' tab to find the library.

The Perkins Library at the University of Southampton is a specialist collection of books on agricultural history: www.southampton.ac.uk/archives.

Family History Library
This is where the genealogical records gathered by the Church of Jesus Christ of Latter Day Saints (the Mormons) are stored. It is in Salt Lake City in the United States, but there are branches around the world called Family History Centres: there are about eighty of them in England. Their locations are given on the website www.familysearch.org. The same site gives access to the International Genealogical Index maintained by the church, containing transcripts of many parish registers.

Society of Genealogists
The library of the Society of Genealogists holds genealogies, both published and unpublished, along with research notes and other papers deposited by family history researchers. Copies of parish registers, poll books and other documents are also held. The society makes a charge to non-members, making it worth checking the online catalogue before a visit. This can be found through www.sog.org.uk. The library is near the Barbican, London.

Museums
Most of the sources discussed in this book have been documentary, but it is well worth remembering the objects associated with the lives our rural ancestors led. Study of the things with which people were surrounded can give us different insights into the way our forebears lived. Some of these things we perhaps have amongst family possessions, as I have my grandfather's baking scales, but most, of course, have passed out of our lives.

There are many museums with collections relating to rural life. Several are specialists in this field, the premier ones being the Museum of English Rural Life and St Fagan's National History Museum, near Cardiff (it used to be known as the Welsh Folk Museum). There are several regional museums, of which the following is a small selection:

Beamish North of England Open Air Museum
Museum of Lincolnshire Life, Lincoln
Museum of East Anglian Life, Stowmarket
Chiltern Open Air Museum, Chalfont St Giles
Vale and Downland Museum, Wantage
Kent Life (formerly Museum of Kent Life), near Maidstone

Ryedale Folk Museum, Hutton le Hole, Yorkshire
Weald and Downland Open Air Museum, Singleton, Sussex
Somerset Rural Life Museum, Glastonbury

All these and other local museums are well worth a visit. As one might expect, the bulk of their collections dates from the late-eighteenth century onwards, since the survival rate for objects is much stronger from that time onwards. As well as all the objects on display, the museums have additional collections in reserve store, which can usually be viewed by appointment. Many also have collections of photographs, and some have collections of archives. To consult their collections, book an appointment in the same way as you would for a record office.

The Rural Museums Network is a co-ordinating group for the specialist museums.

Local history societies
The range of local history societies is considerable. Some cater for local family history studies, some concentrate on particular parishes, while

Some of the horse-drawn farm implements on display at the Museum of English Rural Life. (The author)

others have a wider remit for a county or region. There are online directories to help you find a local society. The Federation of Family History Societies has a list of its constituent societies: www.ffhs.org.uk. Local History Online (www.local-history.co.uk) has a list of local history societies.

As well as joining a society local to your area of interest, the publications and websites of societies in other areas can provide useful leads for ancestors who perhaps moved to another district. Some societies have online discussion forums. Posting a question may produce useful replies from members of the society.

Internet sources

There is an enormous amount of material available through the internet, rendering it all but indispensable as a tool for information now. Every record office has its website, which gives its address, telephone number and opening times; information about the collections is also there, and many have an online catalogue. There are searchable databases, and even the full texts of documents. Indeed, there is so much that it is easy to get carried away into thinking everything is, or should be, available on a website. In fact, of course, most documents are not available for consultation that way, and most library and archive catalogues do not have all their holdings online. Many of the websites offer limited access without payment; many record offices and libraries are subscribers to these sites, which is a help for those uncomfortable with making payments over the internet.

The Church of Jesus Christ of Latter-day Saints (the Mormons), as mentioned above, has been gathering genealogical data from around the world for several years. Much of this can be seen free of charge through their website www.familysearch.org.

Among the leading subscription services are Ancestry.co.uk, Find my Past and Origins Network. All offer a range of databases, including censuses and births, marriages and deaths registers. They also provide services to help in the creation of family trees, including online software. Find my Past now hosts databases formerly run by the Federation of Family History Societies on Family History Online. www.findmypast. co.uk.

Sites that are free to use include Explore Genealogy (www.explore genealogy.co.uk) which contains articles and guides to a wide range of sources. GENUKI (UK and Ireland Genealogy) describes itself as a 'virtual reference library' of genealogical information. The site contains links to databases and references, together with some copies from primary source material and published papers. www.genuki.org.

British History Online is a digital library of some of the core printed primary and secondary sources for the medieval and modern history of the British Isles, compiled by the Institute of Historical Research and the History of Parliament Trust. A wide range of resources has been made available, including many parts of the Victoria County History series, samples of lay subsidy returns, churchwardens' accounts, and so on. Searching via search engines often brings up some of the material held in the databases. The home page is www.british-history.ac.uk.

For an introduction to sources for medieval genealogy, www.medieval genealogy.org.uk provides a comprehensive guide.

Chapter 11

TO CONTINUE …

Clearly the sky's the limit when it comes to researching the life and times of our rural ancestors. In this book there have been many subjects to which only the slightest reference has been made, but which we might want to explore. If the inclination takes us, we can delve further into the way village life worked, taking us into aspects of local history. After all, where does family history end and local history begin? Farming life, the life of the labourers or the rural poor, the rural crafts – all could be subjects that might inspire. And what about the folklore of the country?

I hope enough has been said to encourage the search and maybe more, in seeking out the story of our families. And if you find records in need of a home, talk to an archivist, who will be able to advise what best to do with them.

BIBLIOGRAPHY

This bibliography lists all the books mentioned in the text together with other suggestions for further reading.

General
Introductions to family history
Anthony Adolph, *Tracing Your Family History* (2008)
Nick Barratt, *Nick Barratt's Guide to Your Ancestors' Lives* (Pen and Sword 2010)
David Hey, *The Oxford Guide to Family History* (1993)
David Hey, ed, *The Oxford Companion to Local and Family History* (new ed. 2010)
David Hey, *The Oxford Dictionary of Local and Family History* (1997)
Simon Fowler, *Tracing Your Ancestors* (2011)
Mark Pearsall, *Family history companion: fast-forward your family history search* (2007)
Starting out in Family History (Pen and Sword 2010)
Dan Waddell, *Who do you think you are: the essential guide to tracing your family history* (2004)
Margaret Ward, *Starting Your Family History* (new ed. 2009)

Family history magazines and journals
There are a number of magazines to help the family historian. They include:

Family History Monthly
Family Tree Magazine
Practical Family History
Who Do You Think You Are?
Your Family History
Your Family Tree

Rural literature
Jane Austen, *Emma* (1815, and subsequent editions)
William Cobbett, *Rural Rides* (1830, and subsequent editions)
William Cobbett, *Cottage Economy* (1822, and subsequent editions)
George Eliot, *Middlemarch* (1860, and subsequent editions)
George Eliot, *The Mill on the Floss* (1872, and subsequent editions)
Flora Thompson, *Lark Rise to Candleford* (1945)

Chapter 1: The nature of country society
B J Davey, *Ashwell, 1830–1914: the decline of a village community* (1980)
Christopher Dyer, *Making a Living in the Middle Ages* (2003)
Heckington in the Eighteen Seventies (Heckington Village Trust, 1979)
Pamela Horn, *The Changing Countryside in Victorian and Edwardian England and Wales* (1984)
Alun Howkins, *The Death of Rural England: a social history of the countryside since 1900* (2003)
G E Mingay, *A Social History of the English Countryside* (1990)
Richard Muir, *How to Read a Village* (2007)
R J Olney, ed, *Labouring Life on the Lincolnshire Wolds* (1975)
Zvi Razi, *Life Marriage and Death in a Medieval Parish* (1980)
Victoria County History: various volumes for individual counties.
Joyce Youings, *Sixteenth-century England: the Penguin social history of Britain* (1984)

Chapter 2: Labourers and farm workers
Joseph Arch, *The Story of His Life Told by Himself* (1898)
Alan Armstrong, *Farmworkers: a social and economic history 1770–1980* (1988)
Thomas Hardy, *Far from the Madding Crowd* (1874 and subsequent editions)
Report of the Select Committee on Labourers' Wages, Parliamentary Papers, 1824, vol. VI
Charles Vancouver, *General View of the County of Devon* (1808)
Nicola Verdon, *Rural Women Workers in Nineteenth-century England* (2002)
Ian H Waller, *My Ancestor was an Agricultural Labourer*

Chapter 3: Farmers
Hugh Barrett, *A Good Living* (2000)
Alex Langlands, Peter Ginn and Ruth Goodman, *Victorian Farm* (2008)

Primrose McConnell, *Diary of a Working Farmer* (1906)

Guy Smith, *From Campbell to Kendall: a history of the NFU* (2008)

Brian Short, Charles Watkins, William Foot and Phil Kinsman, *The National Farm Survey 1941–1943* (2000)

Chapter 4: The landowners

Burke's *Landed Gentry* various editions

Burke's *Peerage* various editions

GEC, *The Complete Peerage*

Norman Davis, ed, *Paston Letters and Papers of the Fifteenth Century*, 3 vols (2004)

Mark Girouard, *Life in the English Country House* (1978)

G E Mingay, *English Landed Society in the Eighteenth Century* (1963)

G E Mingay, *The Gentry: the rise and fall of a ruling class* (1976)

Roger North, *The Lives of the Norths* (1890, new edition 1972)

Return of Owners of Land in England and Wales, 1873, Parliamentary Papers, 1874, vol. LXXII.

John Martin Robinson, *The English Country Estate* (1988)

J L Sanford and M Townsend, *The Great Governing Families of England* (1865)

Christopher Simon Sykes, *The Big House* (2004)

F M L Thompson, *English Landed Society in the Nineteenth Century* (1964)

Chapter 5: The great house and estate

Samuel and Sarah Adams, *The Compleat Servant* (1806)

The Banville diaries: journals of a Norfolk gamekeeper, 1822–44, edited by Norma Virgoe and Susan Yaxley; introduction by Lord Buxton (1986)

Thomas Isaac, *The wind in my face: a gamekeeper's memories* (1966)

Kedrun Laurie, *Cricketer Preferred: estate workers at Lyme Park* (1979)

Susanna Wade Martins, *A Great Estate at Work* (1980)

Merlin Waterson, *The Servants Hall* (1980)

John Wilkins, *The autobiography of an English gamekeeper* (1892, new edition 1976)

Chapter 6: Village tradesmen and businessmen

Lin Bensley, *The Village Shop* (2008)

E J T Collins, ed, *Crafts in the English Countryside: towards a future* (2004)

Richard Colyer, *The Welsh cattle drovers: agriculture and the Welsh cattle trade before and during the nineteenth century* (1976)

H E Fitzrandolph and M D Hay, *The Rural Industries of England and Wales* (3 vols, 1926–7)

J Geraint Jenkins, *Traditional Country Craftsmen* (1965)

Una McGovern, *Lost Crafts: rediscovering traditional skills* (2008)

Arthur Randell, *Sixty Years a Fenman* (1966)

George Sturt, *The Wheelwright's Shop* (1923)

Vivien Teasdale, *Tracing Your Textile Ancestors* (Pen and Sword, 2009)

Colin Waters, *A Dictionary of Old Trades, Titles and Occupations* (1999, 2nd ed., 2002)

Chapter 7: Rural Society

The Clerical Guide and Ecclesiastical Directory (1817 and subsequent editions)

Crockford's Clerical Directory (1858 to date)

P Horn, *Education in Rural England 1800–1914* (1978)

George Orwell, *A Clergyman's Daughter* (1935)

J Oxley Parker, *The Oxley Parker Papers from the letters and diaries of an Essex family of land agents in the nineteenth century* (1964)

Chapter 8: Migrants and the poor

Robert Burlison, *Tracing Your Pauper Ancestors* (Pen and Sword, 2009)

Ann Digby, *Pauper Palaces* (1978)

Sir Frederick Eden, *The State of the Poor* (1797)

J Gibson, C Rogers, Cliff Webb, *Poor Law Union Records Vol.1 – South East England and East Anglia* (2nd ed., 1997)

J Gibson, Colin Rogers, *Poor Law Union Records Vol.2 – The Midlands and Northern England* (1993)

J Gibson, Colin Rogers, *Poor Law Union Records Vol. 3 – South-West England, The Marches and Wales* (1993)

J Gibson, F A Youngs Jr, *Poor Law Union Records Vol.4 – Gazetteer and England and Wales* (1993)

Tim Hitchcock, Peter King and Pamela Sharpe, *Chronicling Poverty: the voices and strategies of the English poor, 1640–1840* (1997, 2001)

Steven King, *Poverty and Welfare in England 1700–1850* (2000)

Martin Parsons, *I'll take that one: dispelling the myths of civilian evacuation, 1939–45* (1998)

Thomas Sokoll, *Essex pauper letters, 1731–1837* (2001)

Keith Snell, *Annals of the labouring poor: social change and agrarian England, 1660–1900* (1985)

Chapter 9: Some Records and Sources

Births, marriages and deaths
Cecil R Humphery-Smith, ed, *The Phillimore Atlas and Index of Parish Registers* (1984 and 1995)

Census
Peter Christian & David Annal, *Census: The Expert Guide* (2008)

Churchwardens' accounts
J Charles Cox, *Churchwardens' accounts: from the fourteenth century to the close of the seventeenth century* (1913)
Leighton Bishop, *The General accounts of the churchwardens of Chipping Campden, 1626 to 1907* (Campden Record Series, 1992)

Court records
Mark Bailey (ed.), *The English manor, c.1200–c.1500* (2002)
Ralph Evans, *Manorial economy and society in the later middle ages: selected documents in English translation* (University of Oxford, Department for Continuing Education, 1998)

Diaries and reminiscences
John Burnett, ed, *Useful Toil: autobiographies of working people from the 1820s to the 1920s* (1974)
Reg Dobbs, *The Oldest Young Farmer: the life of a Lincolnshire farmer* (2007)
Thomas Frost, *Reminiscences of a Country Journalist* (1886)
John Heath, ed., *Diaries of Henry Hill of Slackfields Farm 1872–1896* (1982)
Fred Kitchen, *Brother to the Ox: the autobiography of a farm labourer* (1942)
Ann Kussmaul, ed, *The Autobiography of Joseph Mayett of Quainton (1783–1839)* (Buckinghamshire Record Society, 1986)
Mary Russell Mitford, *Our Village* (1824–32, and later editions)
Arthur Randall, *Sixty Years a Fenman* (1966)
Jean Stovin, ed., *Journals of a Methodist Farmer 1871–1875* (1982)

Oral History
George Ewart Evans, *Ask the Fellows Who Cut the Hay* (1956)
Hilary Heffernan, *Voices of Kent and East Sussex Hop Pickers* (2004)
Charles Kightly, *Country Voices: life and lore in farm and village* (1984)
Gilda O'Neill, *Pull No More Bines: an oral history of East London women hop pickers* (1990)

Enclosure records
Steven Hollowell, *Enclosure Records for Historians* (2000)
Roger J P Kain, John Chapman and Richard Oliver, *The Enclosure Maps of England and Wales, 1595–1918* (2004)

Farm records
G E Fussell, ed, *Robert Loder's Farm Accounts 1610–1620* (Camden Society, 3rd series, v. 53, 1936)

Farmers' clubs and agricultural societies
N Goddard, *Harvests of Change: the Royal Agricultural Society of England 1838–1988* (1988)
K Hudson, *The Bath and West: a bicentenary history* (1976)
Kerr Kirkwood, *History of the Wokingham Agricultural Association: the first 150 years* (2005)

Friendly societies
Simon Cordery, *British Friendly Societies 1750–1914* (2003)
Richard Logan, *An Introduction to Friendly Society Records* (2000)

Hearth Tax
J Gibson, *The Hearth Tax and other later Stuart Tax Lists* (1996)
Elizabeth Parkinson, *The Establishment of the Hearth Tax 1662–66* (2008)

Maps
G Beech and R Mitchell, *Maps for Family and Local History: the records of the tithe, Valuation Office and farm management surveys* (2004)

Poll tax
Carolyn C. Fenwick, ed, *The Poll Tax Returns of 1377, 1379 and 1381* (1994, 2001, 2005)

Probate inventories
Jill Groves, ed, *Bowden Wills: wills and probate inventories from a Cheshire township, Part 1, 1600–1650* (1997)
Mark Overton, *A Bibliography of British Probate Inventories* (1983)

Quarter Sessions
Jeremy Gibson, *Quarter Sessions Records for Family Historians* (1995)

Tithe
Roger J P Kain and Hugh C Prince, *Tithe Surveys* (2000)
Roger J P Kain and Richard R Oliver, *The Tithe Maps of England and Wales – a cartographic analysis and county-by-county catalogue* (1995).

Wills
Jeremy Gibson, *Wills and where to find them* (1974)

Chapter 10: Where to find the information
Archive sources
A good general introduction to family history and its sources is David Hey, *Journeys in Family History: the National Archives guide to exploring your past, finding your ancestors* (2004).

The internet might be full of information about sources, but there is still room for a printed guide. Janet Foster and Julia Sheppard, *British Archives: a guide to archive sources in the United Kingdom* (4th ed, 2002)

Local history
Peter Edwards, *Rural Life: guide to local records* (1993)
Peter Edwards, *Farming: guide to local records* (1991)

Most local family history societies publish their own newsletters and journals, many of which contain articles of substance. You need to join the society to receive these, of course.

Internet sources

Guides to using online sources
Nick Barratt, ed, *Researching Your Family History Online* (2nd ed, 2009)
Peter Christian, *The Genealogist's Internet* (4th ed. 2009)
Graeme Davis, *Your Family Tree Online* (2009)
Chris Paton, *Tracing Your Ancestors on the Internet* (2011)
Colin Waters, *Family History on the Net 2009–10* (2009)

Websites
All the websites mentioned in the text are listed here. All were active when checked in the late summer of 2010. All internet addresses begin

with http://. This prefix is only included below when it is followed by something other than the most common www.

Access to Archives: www.nationalarchives.gov.uk/a2a
Ancestry.co.uk: www.ancestry.co.uk
Archon record offices directory: www.nationalarchives.gov.uk/archon
Bodleian Library, University of Oxford: www.bodley.ox.ac.uk
British History Online: www.british-history.ac.uk.
British Library: www.bl.uk
British newspaper library, Colindale: http://newspapers.bl.uk/blcs
Census 1881: www.freebmd.org.uk.
Chadwyck-Healey, House of Commons papers: http://parlipapers.
  chadwyck.co.uk/marketing/index.jsp.
Explore Genealogy: www.exploregenealogy.co.uk.
Federation of Family History Societies: www.ffhs.org.uk
Find my Past: www.findmypast.co.uk
Freebmd: www.freebmd.org.uk
Freereg: www.freereg.org.uk
Friendly Societies Research Group: www.open.ac.uk/socialsciences/
  friendly-societies-research-group/
General Register Office certificate services: www.ips.gov.uk
GENUKI: www.genuki.org
Historical directories project: www.historicaldirectories.org
HM Courts Service: www.hmcourts-service.gov.uk/infoabout/civil/
  probate/index.htm.
International Genealogical Index: www.familysearch.org
Internet Archive: www.archive.org
Local History Online: www.local-history.co.uk.
Medieval genealogy: www.medievalgenealogy.org.uk
Mills Archive Trust: www.millsarchive.com
Modern Records Centre, University of Warwick: http://modernrecords.
  warwick.ac.uk
Mormon church: www.familysearch.org.
Museum of English Rural Life: www.reading.ac.uk/merl
Old Maps: www.old-maps.co.uk
Origins Network: www.origins.net
The National Archives: www.nationalarchives.gov.uk
The National Archives documents online: www.nationalarchives.gov.uk/
  documentsonline

National Register of Archives: www.nationalarchives.gov.uk/nra

New Landscapes, Berkshire enclosure awards: www.berkshireen closure.org.uk

Newsplan, East Midlands newspapers: http://newsplan.liem.org.uk

Parliamentary Papers guide: www.bl.uk/reshelp/findhelprestype/offpubs/ukofficalpub/parlpapers/parliamentpapers.pdf

Romany and Traveller Family History Society: www.rtfhs.org.uk

Rossbret institutions: www.institutions.org.uk

Royal Agricultural Society of England: www.rase.org.uk

Society of Genealogists: www.sog.org.uk

Suffolk Record Office: www.suffolk.gov.uk/LeisureAndCulture/Local HistoryAndHeritage/SuffolkRecordOffice

Sussex Record Society www.sussexrecordsociety.org.uk

University of Southampton, Perkins Library: www.southampton.ac.uk/archives.

Wikipedia, the online encyclopaedia, is useful for background reference. This is the home page: http://en.wikipedia.org/wiki/Main_Page

INDEX

herdsman 28
Herefordshire 47
Hertfordshire 28, 44, 107
Hey, David 51
higgler 71
Hilliard, Robert 43
hind 20
hiring fair 17–9, 20, 30, 122
hiring, annual 25, 26
hops 24–5
horsemen 15–7, 19, 21, 22, 28
House of Lords Record Office 110
household accounts 56, 112
housekeeper 58, 59, 60
huckster 70
Humber valley 24
Huntingdonshire 8, 28, 124
husbandman 43, 44, 45, 47

Imperial War Museum 31
industrial towns 89
industrial workers 23
industrialization 8, 9, 10, 95
industry 22, 63, 64, 109
industry, rural 7, 62, 63–5, 79
Inland Revenue 10, 63
innkeeper 48
Inquisitions post-mortem 117
International Genealogical Index 139
internet 56, 96, 103, 124, 135, 137, 138, 141
Irish harvesters 24, 93
ironmonger 71
itinerant labour 23, 24, 93
itinerant traders 67, 69–70, 71

Jefferies, Richard 36
Jones, David 76
Jones, George 44

Kelly, Frederick, directories 108–9
Kent 15, 24, 25, 43, 55, 58, 89, 120, 139
Kiddington, Oxon 44
Kilburn, Yorks 72
King, Gregory 10, 13, 33, 94

King's Lynn 74
Kirdford, Sussex 7
kitchen maid 60
Kitchen, Fred 21

labourer, agricultural 1, 2, 6, 7, 8, 11, 13–31, 33, 36, 40, 43, 44, 45, 46, 47, 73, 82, 87, 92, 93, 97, 106, 107, 110, 122, 129, 133, 142
labourers, day 21, 22
labourers, general 65, 102
labourers, outdoor 13, 21–2
labourers, sources 30
labourers, wages 94
Lancashire 16, 24, 87, 100
land agent: see Estate agent
land tax 49, 117, 129
land tenure 37–8
landed interest 51
landowners 2, 7, 34, 38, 39, 43, 44, 46, 51–6, 57, 58, 81, 82, 83, 86, 89, 110, 111, 112, 113, 117, 118, 122, 131, 137
Law of Property Act 104
leasehold tenure 38, 48, 57, 103, 104, 118
libraries 138–9
Lincoln Rutland & Stamford Mercury 124
Lincolnshire 5, 7, 15, 19, 21, 36, 39, 40, 41, 42, 52, 53, 62, 63, 65, 70, 71, 72, 74, 75, 84, 106, 115, 118, 124
local history societies 103, 140–1
local studies libraries 5, 101, 107, 109, 124, 135, 138
Loder, Robert 43, 113
lord of the manor 45, 103, 116, 118

magistrate 24, 31, 82, 97
malting 65, 93, 109
manorial courts 103, 104
Manorial Documents Register 104
manorial records 49, 77, 118–20
manorial rolls 30, 105
manorial surveys 130
maps 30, 43, 49, 50, 84, 105, 109, 110, 120–2, 130, 138

158